Storage

The many racks and closets and bins that provide the essential storage for everything from umbrellas to checkerboards are also important elements in the décor of your home — as the portfolio on the following pages illustrates. And storage units should measure up to the standards of taste you have set for the rest of your home.

The basic plans for storage units will be determined, of course, by their utility, but their appearance can be elegant, rustic, avant-garde, classic or informal — whatever style you choose. Sizes and shapes can be modified within the constraints of space. Color can become an arresting accent or a subtle bridge blending the elements of a room together. You can mix or match textures and materials; you can select harmonious or contrasting hardware and woodwork, or omit both kinds of ornamental touches in favor of a sleek contemporary look.

Starting on page 12 with the fundamentals of planning, this volume presents a step-by-step guide to creating an array of storage units. Build them just as they are shown here if you choose, or give your imagination free rein to conjure personalized projects that do full justice to your special style.

Sleek see-through boxes — a few with smoky-plastic doors — are stacked one upon another to create a decorative storage wall downstairs; more boxes are arranged as a

bookshelf-balcony rail for the sleeping loft. Most boxes are plain square frames; inner shelves preserve the cubic effect in double- and quadruple-length versions.

Classic paneled doors, chosen to complement existing woodwork, open onto highly functional storage for outdoor gear: sports equipment, toys, galoshes and coats.

Flush doors and hidden hinges give a smooth face to cleverly designed cabinets for a family's footwear. Slots atop and alongside the units act as grips for opening them.

Boxes that move on polystyrene skids are the building blocks of a superscale storage unit in this studio loft. Packing-blanket upholstery on the near boxes turns them

into a generous lounge and brings a welcome splash of color. Stacked boxes form shelves behind a banquette for dining at the far left and a couch to the right.

Other Publications:
THE ENCHANTED WORLD
THE KODAK LIBRARY OF CREATIVE PHOTOGRAPHY
GREAT MEALS IN MINUTES
THE CIVIL WAR
PLANET EARTH
COLLECTOR'S LIBRARY OF THE CIVIL WAR
LIBRARY OF HEALTH
CLASSICS OF THE OLD WEST
THE EPIC OF FLIGHT
THE GOOD COOK
THE SEAFARERS
WORLD WAR II
HOME REPAIR AND IMPROVEMENT
THE OLD WEST
LIFE LIBRARY OF PHOTOGRAPHY (revised)
LIFE SCIENCE LIBRARY (revised)

*For information on and a full
description of any of the Time-Life Books
series listed above, please write:*
Reader Information
Time-Life Books
541 North Fairbanks Court
Chicago, Illinois 60611

This volume is one of a series that features home decorating projects.

Storage

by the Editors of Time-Life Books

TIME-LIFE BOOKS □ ALEXANDRIA, VIRGINIA

YOUR HOME

SERIES DIRECTOR: Gerry Schremp
Deputy Director: Adrian Allen
Picture Editor: Marion F. Briggs
Designer: Raymond Ripper
Chief Researcher: Barbara Levitt
Editorial Staff for *Storage*
Text Editors: Jim Hicks, Peter Pocock,
David Thiemann
Staff Writers: Adrienne George, Adrianne
Goodman, Karin Kinney, Denise Li, Glenn Martin
McNatt, Jane A. Martin, William Worsley
Assistant Designer: Susan K. White
Copy Coordinator: Robert M. S. Somerville
Picture Coordinator: Renée DeSandies
Editorial Assistant: Carolyn Wall Halbach

Special Contributors: Lynn R. Addison, William
Doyle, Jennifer B. Gilman, Leon Greene, Karen J.
Jensen, Kathleen M. Kiely, Wendy Murphy,
Mark M. Steele

Editorial Operations
Design: Ellen Robling (assistant director)
Copy Room: Diane Ullius
Production: Anne B. Landry (director),
Celia Beattie
Quality Control: James J. Cox (director),
Sally Collins
Library: Louise D. Forstall

Correspondents: Elisabeth Kraemer-Singh (Bonn);
Margot Hapgood, Dorothy Bacon (London);
Miriam Hsia (New York); Maria Vincenza Aloisi,
Josephine du Brusle (Paris); Ann Natanson
(Rome). Valuable assistance was also provided by:
Carolyn Chubet, Christina Lieberman (New York);
Ann Wise (Rome).

THE CONSULTANT

Frederick L. Wall, a furniture maker and sculptor,
is an instructor in furniture design at the Corcoran
School of Art in Washington, D.C. His work has
been featured in many exhibits and publications.
Mr. Wall is responsible for designing and building
many of the projects shown in this volume.

First printing. Printed in U.S.A.
Published simultaneously in Canada.
School and library distribution by Silver Burdett
Company, Morristown, New Jersey 07960.

TIME-LIFE is a trademark of
Time Incorporated U.S.A.

Library of Congress Cataloguing in
Publication Data
Main entry under title:
Storage.

   (Your home)
   Includes index.
   1. Storage in the home. 2. Do-it-yourself work.
I. Time-Life Books.   II. Series: Your
home (Alexandria, Va.).
RX309.S76 1985   643'.52   84-16144
ISBN 0-8094-5508-0
ISBN 0-8094-5509-9 (lib. bdg.)

CONTENTS

The closet: A paradigm of well-planned storage

Having "a place for everything and everything in its place" is a Victorian ideal almost everyone shares. But storing a family's many belongings in an orderly fashion can be as challenging as putting together a jigsaw puzzle: There are so many sizes and shapes, and at first it would seem impossible to fit them all into the space available. With planning, however, a place can be found into which each piece slips easily. Finding those places and matching them to a profusion of clothes, books, tools and toys is the theme of this volume.

The first chapter deals with closets, from the drawing of plans through construction and installation. The following chapter about racks starts with the garage and travels through the house, featuring a wood peg rack, a hall tree, and fabric racks for hobbyists' collections and children's trinkets. The final chapter is devoted to boxes ranging from the simplest of basic cubes to a high-technology acrylic-plastic case for video cassettes.

All of these projects are ones you can undertake by yourself. And all of them can be modified to suit your particular needs and tastes. Therefore, devising solutions for your problems begins with analyzing available space and the objects to be stored there. The space may be an existing storage area, such as a closet or cupboard, that can be improved. Or it may be neglected space: an empty wall, the back of a door, the area under a stairway.

Some objects may be kept in plain sight because they look decorative — as the aggregation of sewing paraphernalia on page 52 illustrates. Most objects, though, are best hidden behind doors or under a lid such as that on the boot bin on page 92.

Whatever the space available, fitting objects into it depends on matching measurements — as demonstrated by the closets at right and on the following pages. Here, closets are compartmentalized to make every inch of space perform a special job.

All these closets are 2 feet deep and have folding doors. Closets of other sizes and shapes can be divided similarly; swinging doors would offer space for hooks or racks.

Designing a closet begins with exact measurements and scale views drawn on graph paper. A front view of each wall on which you plan to hang rods or shelves is essential; use side views to check the depth of compartments, especially where shelves extend to different distances.

Next, gather all the items you hope to fit into the closet and measure them, noting width, length and thickness. Measure hanging garments on hangers and suspended from a rod; foldable objects such as sweaters, towels and bed linen will of course be measured while they are folded.

Architects and interior designers use standard dimensions for wearing apparel when they do preliminary closet layouts; these, to a great extent, are the measurements shown here. However, clothes' sizes and styles are far from standard: A cable-stitched sweater takes more space than a cashmere sweater — and objects can be hung or folded in so many different ways that only the dimensions you take are a sure basis for planning.

Closet shops, lumberyards, home centers and hardware stores furnish a wide variety of rods, drawers, racks and shelves; check on these and note their dimensions. Then, using the measurements of your possessions as a guide, sketch rods and shelves and drawers into your plan. Store-bought units come with installation directions. Homemade rods and shelves can be put up in various ways, as this chapter shows.

Although the rules are flexible, professional designers have a number of guidelines that will help you create your personal plans:
● Allow ¾ inch in your plans for the thickness of each particleboard, plywood or 1-by-12 shelf or partition you draw. In the designs here, all measurements are rounded off; your plan may show a lot of fractions.
● Measure and allow space for glides that hold drawers or sliding baskets, and for sockets that hold clothes rods.
● Allow a 3-inch clearance from a rod to a shelf above it.
● When measuring hanging clothes, allow 3 inches for the hanger from the top of the garment to the clothes rod.
● Because most hangers are 16 to 18 inches wide, hang the clothes rod about 12 inches from the back wall to allow for the thickness of the garment and a 2-inch clearance.

A HOSPITABLE HALL CLOSET

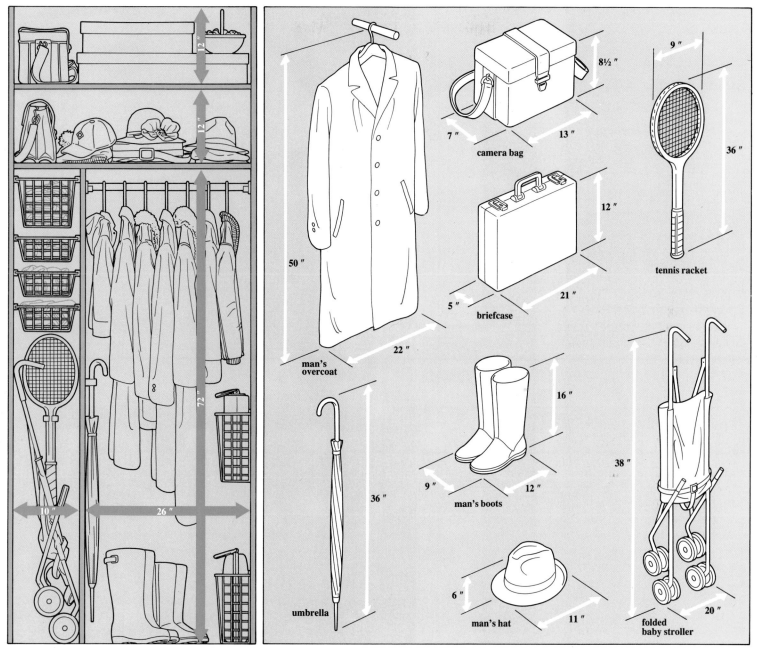

This head-on view shows how much paraphernalia can be stowed neatly in a closet 2 feet deep, 3 feet wide and 8 feet high. Achieving such a goal requires measuring everything that will go into the closet — the sampling at right is typical — and planning the closet rods, shelves, racks, drawers, hooks, clamps and clips accordingly. Depending on their thickness, six to 10 coats or jackets would fit in the hanging space allotted here; seven are shown. The clothes rod is set 69 inches above the floor — 63 inches is standard — to allow space below for high boots and overshoes. On the wall to the right of the coats are vinyl-coated wire baskets holding briefcases; to the left, gripper clips hold umbrellas. A 10-inch-wide compartment beside the hanging space supports four wire baskets on glides to hold mufflers, caps, mittens and such. The baskets, glides and gripper clips all are available where closet supplies are sold. Below the sliding baskets a tennis racket is clipped to the wall and a folded stroller stands on the floor. Across the top, two shelves hold hats, purses, storage boxes and a camera bag.

A COMMODIOUS WOMAN'S CLOSET

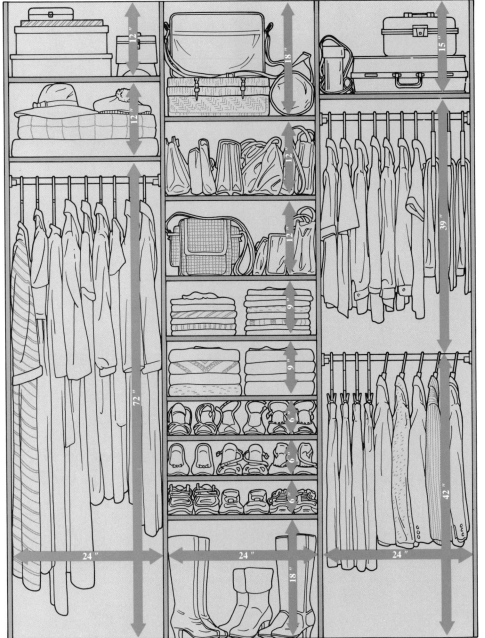

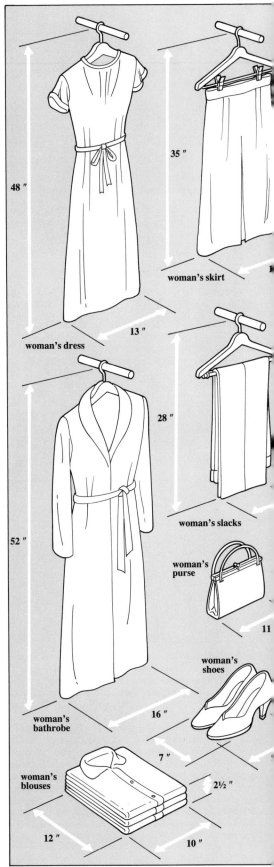

Clothes rods at three different heights (above) provide hanging space tailored to clothes of different lengths. At the left-hand side of the closet a rod 69 inches above the floor holds long gowns, robes, coats and dresses. At the right-hand side, a rod 42 inches above the floor holds jackets and skirts, and another rod above it has the 36-inch clearance needed here for blouses and folded slacks. All the rods are set about 12 inches from the rear wall to allow 2 inches or so of clearance there.

Between the rods, shelves 12 inches deep — as measured from front to back — and approximately 24 inches wide hold three pairs of shoes apiece; the shelves need only be 6 inches apart because tall boots stand on the floor below them in a compartment 18 inches high. Above the shoes are stacks of folded blouses and sweaters, purses, small suitcases, even a picnic basket. Hats, luggage and boxes of out-of-season clothing fill the shelves over the rods — shelves carefully spaced to allow 3 inches of clearance between their bottom faces and the rods. Like the other measurements shown in the closet design above and at right, the heights of these shelves have been rounded off to whole numbers.

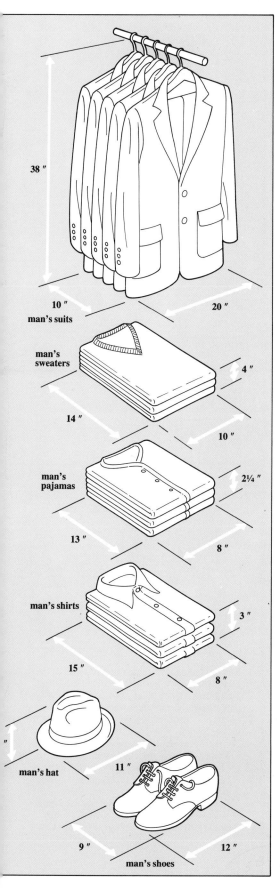

38 "

10 "
man's suits

20 "

man's
sweaters

4 "

14 "

10 "

man's
pajamas

2¼ "

13 "

8 "

man's shirts

3 "

15 "

8 "

man's hat

11 "

9 "

12 "

man's shoes

A CAREFULLY ENGINEERED MAN'S CLOSET

12 "

12 "

12 "

10 "

10 "

10 "

6 "

6 "

24 "

18 "

42 "

42 "

48 "

Two parallel clothes rods increase the hanging space in a closet so that some of its width can be used for shelves. In this 2-by-6-by-8-foot closet, the rods offer a total of about 8 feet of hanging space, and the shelves are approximately 2 feet wide. Here the lower rod, set 42 inches above the floor, holds suits and jackets; the upper rod, with a clearance of 39 inches, holds shirts and pants that are folded over hangers. Straight-hung pants may measure 45 inches or more in length and would require a third rod with a clearance of about 50 inches.

In this design, the three uppermost shelves are about 12 inches deep to support bags, caps and hats. The rest of the shelves are 15 inches deep to accommodate folded shirts, sweaters and pajamas, and to be large enough to hold two pairs of shoes each. A slide-out or swing-out tie rack screwed to the partition between shelves and rods keeps ties neat.

A SCALED-DOWN CHILD'S CLOSET

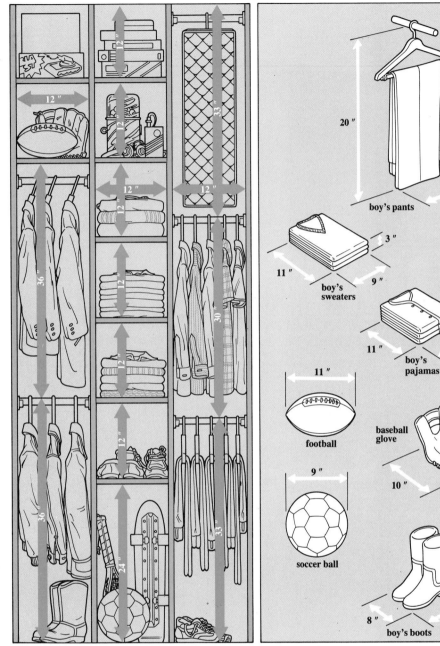

A NEATLY STACKED LINEN CLOSET

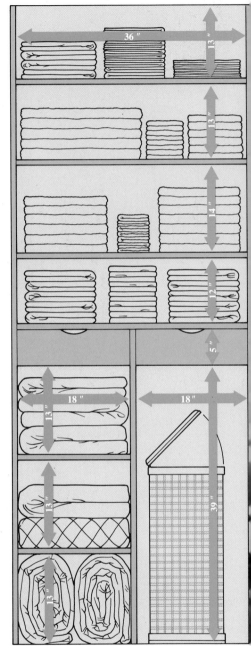

Because children's needs change as they grow, their closets demand maximum flexibility. The small 2-by-3-by-8-foot closet shown here — designed for a 10-year-old boy — incorporates both shelves and clothes rods that can be moved up or down on metal tracks (pages 18-20). Because hangers for children's clothes are small, the rods are set only 8 inches from the wall — freeing space in the front of the closet for racks, hooks or gripper clips on the side walls. Here, four rods help organize a child's wardrobe by offering separate places for dress jackets and coats (top left rod), everyday jackets (bottom left rod), pants (bottom right rod) and shirts (middle right rod). A fifth rod at top right contains a garment bag for out-of-season items. Between the rods are shelves about 12 inches deep for shoes, sweaters, shirts and pajamas — and for assorted games and sports gear. Here, as in the other closets at right, the width and height measurements have been rounded off to whole numbers.

Enough linens for a family of four, with extras for guests, fit comfortably in this 2-by-3-by-8-foot closet. Each shelf in the top half of the closet is shallower than the one below it — the top shelf measures 16 inches from front to back, the next shelf 18 inches, the next 20 inches, the rest 22 inches — to ensure comfortable access to the linens. The distance between shelves is based on the height of their contents, with 2-inch clearances.

Tablecloths and napkins that are used only on special occasions occupy the top shelf; the next two shelves, near eye level, hold

A JOB-ORIENTED CLEANING CLOSET

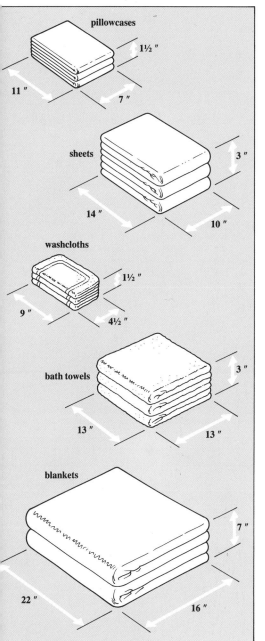

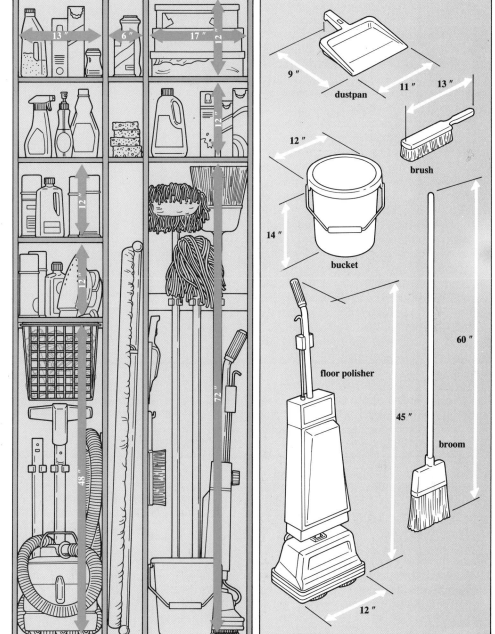

towels and washcloths. The lowest full-width shelf is for sheets and pillowcases. Linens that are folded in other ways than those shown would, of course, call for other basic dimensions.

Wood drawers on glides, available at hardware stores, hang below the bed-linen shelf and contain such supplies as toothpaste, bandages and soap. Fragrant soaps do double duty by spreading their scent through the linens. Blankets and sleeping bags occupy the bottom left section, next to a clothes hamper that slides in and out.

The design of a cleaning closet begins with providing spaces for its most awkward contents: the tall brooms and mops and the bulky ironing board and vacuum cleaner. The remaining space then can be compartmentalized with shelves and drawers as needed. Here, all of the shelves and partitions are 20¾ inches deep to accommodate a capacious store-bought sliding basket that takes full advantage of the 2-foot depth of the closet. The vacuum cleaner shares the compartment with the basket, which holds polishes, brushes and cloths; the cleaner's attachments are hung on the rear wall with gripper clips. The ironing board stays clean in a separate space about 6 inches wide and 6 feet high; the iron is on a shelf beside it. The mops and brooms have a 6-foot-tall compartment where they can be clipped flat against the rear wall; a dustpan and brush hang from clips on the middle partition; a floor polisher and pail share the floor space. Items on the shelves above are arranged for convenience: Cleaners and sprays used for the same job or room are stored together to simplify finding supplies and keeping an inventory of them.

Easily adjustable clothes rods

Clothes rods are a closet's centerpiece, the starting point for rational remodeling. Because a rod's placement determines the design of a closet's other parts — racks, shelves, drawers and the like — an adjustable rod system expands the design options for the entire space.

The versatile system installed here can accommodate one rod or several, and the height of each rod can be varied to keep pace with growing children or with changing fashions. The system's simple hardware can also be used to augment a clothes rod with tiers of adjustable shelves (*box, page 20*).

An adjustable system has four components (*top right*). Metal standards, which are available in 1-foot increments and should be at least 5 feet long, are fastened vertically to the closet's side walls. Because the standards ideally are mounted 12 inches from the rear wall, a rare location for wall studs, they generally are backed by well-secured 1-by-4 uprights that rest on the baseboard. To support the rod or rods, U-shaped metal brackets clip into horizontal slots in each standard. And the rod itself is a $1\frac{1}{16}$-inch steel pipe with walls $\frac{1}{8}$ inch thick, sheathed in stainless steel or chrome.

All of this hardware is available from closet-accessories shops or builder's-hardware stores. The dealer usually will cut the rod to length with a heavy-duty pipe cutter, although in a pinch you can do the job at home with a hacksaw. To determine the rod's length, measure between the closet's side walls and subtract $2\frac{1}{8}$ inches if the standards will be fastened to uprights, $\frac{5}{8}$ inch if they will be fastened directly to the walls.

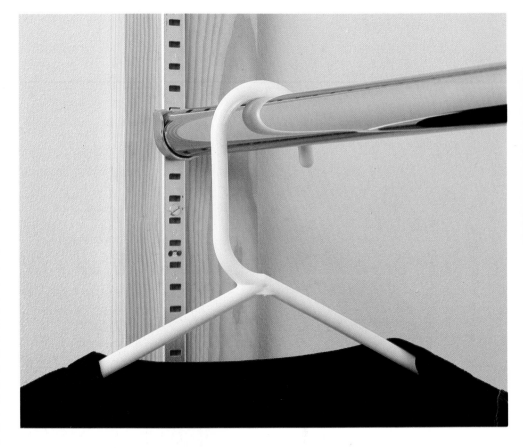

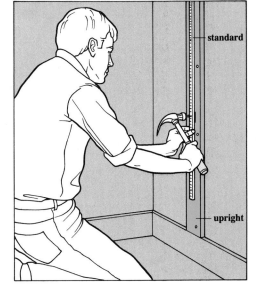

3 Aligning the uprights. Near the top of each side wall, make a vertical tick mark 10 inches from the closet's back wall. Cut two 1-by-4s to fit between the ceiling or ceiling molding and the baseboard. Set one board at a time vertically against a side wall, aligning its rear edge with the mark, and fasten it temporarily with a nail driven through the board opposite the mark. Hold a carpenter's level against the board's edge, pivot the board until it is plumb (*right*) and fasten the upright's lower end with a second temporary nail. Permanently attach both uprights with fasteners suited to the wall's structure (*pages 124-125*). Pull out the temporary nails.

standard

upright

4 Mounting the first standard. About 2 and 6 feet above the floor, make vertical pencil marks on each upright $1\frac{1}{2}$ inches from its front edge. Place a standard along one upright, aligning its front edge with the marks and setting its bottom 8 to 10 inches above the floor. Fasten the standard with temporary nails driven through its screw holes opposite the top and bottom marks.

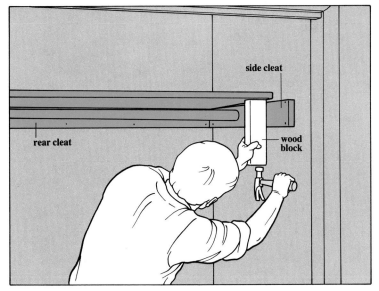

1 **Removing the shelf.** If the old clothes rod sits in slots or screw-on brackets and can be lifted out easily, do so; otherwise leave it in place for the moment. Unnail the shelf atop the cleats by holding a wood block against its underside next to each cleat in turn and driving the block and shelf upward with a hammer. Remove the shelf and set it aside.

2 **Removing the cleats.** Slip a wood chisel's beveled face against the wall beneath the nails at one end of a side cleat and gently pry the cleat's lower edge about ¼ inch from the wall. Slide a pry bar into this gap, place a wood block behind the bar for leverage and pry the cleat away from the wall. Pull the cleat out of the closet along with the old rod, if it was not removed in Step 1. Then pry away the other side cleat and the rear cleat, if any. Patch the nail holes in the wall with spackling compound.

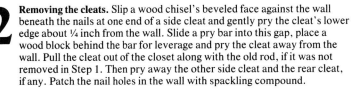

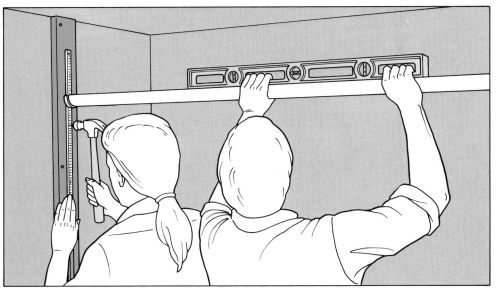

5 **Fastening the standard.** Use a ⅟₁₆-inch twist bit to drill pilot holes for ¾-inch No. 6 screws through each of the standard's screw holes. Screw the standard to the upright. As you proceed, remove the temporary nails and replace them with screws.

6 **Leveling the standards.** Attach rod brackets at matching positions on the mounted and unmounted standards, using each standard's numbered slots as a guide. Hold the unmounted standard against the vertical pencil marks on its upright while a helper puts the new clothes rod on the brackets and holds a carpenter's level atop the center of the rod. Move the standard vertically until the rod is level, then tap temporary nails into two of its screw holes. Remove the rod and permanently fasten the second standard (*Step 5*). Install rods at the appropriate heights for your closet (*pages 12-17*), and from them suspend clothes hangers with the longest garments intended for each rod; reposition the brackets if there is less than 3 inches of clearance beneath the longest garment.

Adding Adjustable Shelves

Like adjustable clothes rods, movable shelves increase the flexibility of any closet design. The shelves at right are a simple extension of the clothes-rod system shown overleaf, merely requiring a second pair of metal standards for four-corner support. Their installation involves only two small variations in technique. The additional uprights are fitted snugly into the corners, to allow easy fastening to corner studs. And the standards must be carefully leveled (*Step 2*), so that shelves do not wobble on their mounting clips.

The shelves can be made of ¾-inch plywood or particleboard, provided that the edges are filled with spackling compound before the shelves are painted; alternatively, they can be made of 1-inch lumber. Such materials are strong enough to support a light load on a 48-inch-long shelf or a heavy load on a 30-inch shelf. Longer shelves need to be supported by a rear cleat.

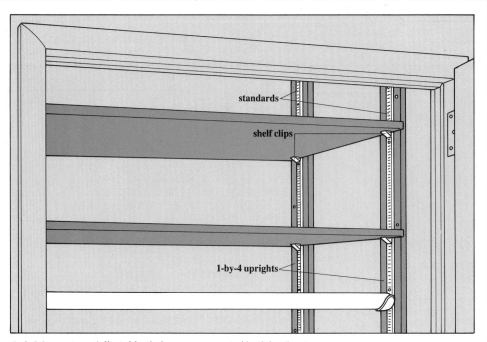

A shelving system. Adjustable shelves are supported both by the standards that hold the clothes rod and by a second pair of standards near the closet's rear corners. The shelves rest on metal clips that fit into each standard's horizontal slots. The front and back edges of each shelf should extend at least 1½ inches beyond the clips, to prevent the shelf from accidentally being knocked off its perch.

1 **Installing the uprights.** Cut a 1-by-4 to fit between the baseboard and the ceiling or ceiling molding at a back corner of the closet. Set this upright vertically on the side wall at the corner. Check the upright with a carpenter's level; if necessary, ease the upright's top or bottom away from the corner until the board is plumb. Temporarily fasten the upright to the wall with nails, then permanently attach it with appropriate fasteners *(pages 124-125)* — typically wood screws driven within 1½ inches of the corner, the usual location of a corner stud. Install another upright at the closet's other back corner.

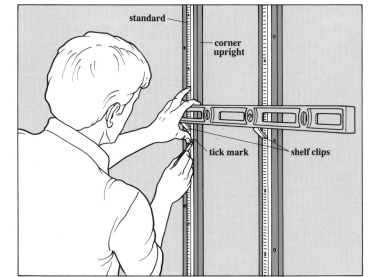

2 **Leveling the standards.** Mark the top and bottom of a corner upright 1 inch from its front edge. Insert shelf clips in the same slot on an unmounted standard and on the already-installed front standard. Hold the unmounted standard against the marks on the upright, and pencil a tick mark on the standard's side below the clip. Hold a carpenter's level on the shelf brackets, and slide the unmounted standard vertically until the clips are level; then opposite the standard's pencil mark make a matching tick mark on the upright *(above)*. Remove the level, align the standard with the marks and fasten it with ¾-inch No. 6 wood screws. Mount the other corner standard in the same way.

Hardware for Fixed Rods

While not as versatile as adjustable rods, fixed clothes rods retain a place in many closets. In an unfinished closet, a fixed rod can be mounted simply in pre-drilled holes when the wood shelf cleats are installed *(pages 32-33)*. But the hardware shown below is more versatile, letting you tailor the fixtures in a finished closet to individual storage needs.

Fixed rods are available in three basic types: the 1¹⁄₁₆-inch pipe shown on page 18; 1¹⁄₁₆-inch chrome-plated steel tubing; and 1³⁄₈-inch wood dowels. Pipe is by far the strongest, spanning up to 6 feet. Steel tubing, which is thin-walled, and wood dowels are cheaper; however, on spans greater than 4 feet they require intermediate supports such as brackets *(below, right)* every 32 inches. Each material requires different cutting tools:

Pipe is best cut by the dealer. Tubing requires a hacksaw or an inexpensive tubing cutter, while wood dowels need a backsaw and miter box.

Except for the tension rod at bottom left, all of the hardware shown here requires anchorage either to a horizontal wood cleat or to wall studs, if they are located conveniently. Ideally the rod should be mounted 12 inches from a closet's rear wall; 9 inches is minimum.

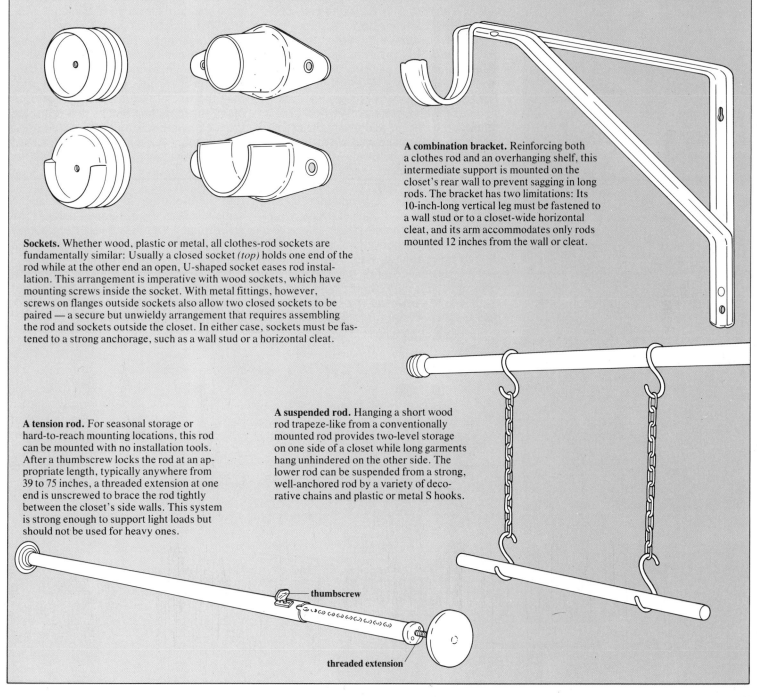

Sockets. Whether wood, plastic or metal, all clothes-rod sockets are fundamentally similar: Usually a closed socket *(top)* holds one end of the rod while at the other end an open, U-shaped socket eases rod installation. This arrangement is imperative with wood sockets, which have mounting screws inside the socket. With metal fittings, however, screws on flanges outside sockets also allow two closed sockets to be paired — a secure but unwieldy arrangement that requires assembling the rod and sockets outside the closet. In either case, sockets must be fastened to a strong anchorage, such as a wall stud or a horizontal cleat.

A combination bracket. Reinforcing both a clothes rod and an overhanging shelf, this intermediate support is mounted on the closet's rear wall to prevent sagging in long rods. The bracket has two limitations: Its 10-inch-long vertical leg must be fastened to a wall stud or to a closet-wide horizontal cleat, and its arm accommodates only rods mounted 12 inches from the wall or cleat.

A tension rod. For seasonal storage or hard-to-reach mounting locations, this rod can be mounted with no installation tools. After a thumbscrew locks the rod at an appropriate length, typically anywhere from 39 to 75 inches, a threaded extension at one end is unscrewed to brace the rod tightly between the closet's side walls. This system is strong enough to support light loads but should not be used for heavy ones.

A suspended rod. Hanging a short wood rod trapeze-like from a conventionally mounted rod provides two-level storage on one side of a closet while long garments hang unhindered on the other side. The lower rod can be suspended from a strong, well-anchored rod by a variety of decorative chains and plastic or metal S hooks.

thumbscrew

threaded extension

An imaginative solution to clutter

The odds and ends often lost in the dark recesses of a closet can be kept close at hand with a door-mounted rack like the one at left. Two rows of dowel pegs near the top hold caps, jackets, bags or a dog's leash; near the bottom, dowels separate compartments for umbrellas, walking sticks or baseball bats. Moreover, this added storage area occupies hardly any space in the closet: The deepest part of the rack protrudes just 3½ inches from the door.

Finished to match the door, the rack blends smoothly into the background. Painted or outlined in a contrasting color, the rack becomes a decorative accent. The frame of the rack is a shallow rectangle of lumber, with a plywood back. Joints at the corners and where the crosspieces attach are secured with glue and screws. The ½-inch dowels used for pegs and for compartment separators fit into holes drilled with the help of a drill guide, which keeps the bit perpendicular.

Because dowel diameters may vary slightly from their nominal size, check before you buy to be sure your dowels will fit their holes snugly. With your drill and a ½-inch bit, make a few holes in a piece of scrap wood; then use the holes to test the fit of the dowels at the store or lumberyard. If necessary, buy larger dowels and sand them down to suit the holes.

Be sure that not only dowels but all of the other parts of the rack as well fit together properly before you glue them in place. At each step, screw the pieces into place; if they fit correctly, unscrew them, give them a final sanding (easier when the pieces are apart), and then apply the glue and reassemble the pieces.

The 16½-by-72-inch rack shown here fits a standard closet door 24 inches wide and 80 inches tall. You can vary the size of the rack, or the number and positions of the dowel blocks, to suit your needs.

You may also need to take the construction of the door into account in planning the size of the rack or the positioning of the mounting blocks that reinforce the rack where screws are used to hold it on the door. A rack mounted on a flat, hollow-core door can be any size that fits and allows the door to close; but a rack on a frame-and-panel door must be built so that the mounting blocks will be at the same levels as the horizontal parts of the solid frame. You may even add another mounting block near the center to attach the rack firmly to the frame.

Choose round-head wood screws to mount the rack on a frame-and-panel door. But choose toggle bolts (*page 125*) if you have a hollow-core door.

Materials List	
1 x 3	23 ' clear pine 1 x 3, cut into: 2 pieces, 72 " long 2 pieces, 16½ " long 6 pieces, 15 " long
Dowels	9 ½ " wood dowels, 3½ " long
Plywood	1 piece ¼ " AC-grade hardwood plywood, 16½ " x 72 "

Screws	32 No. 10 flat-head wood screws, 1½ " long 4 No. 10 round-head wood screws, 3 " long, or 4 2-inch toggle bolts (to mount rack to door)
Nails	about 30 panel nails, 1 " long
Glue	wood glue
Paint	latex primer and latex semigloss paint

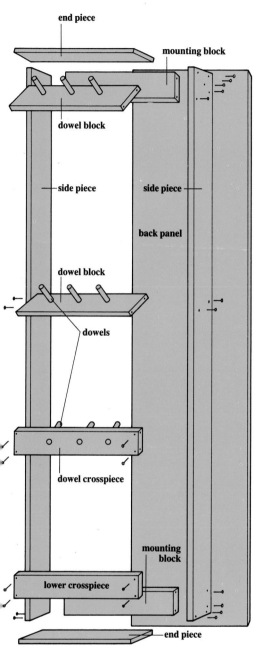

end piece

mounting block

dowel block

side piece   **side piece**

back panel

dowel block

dowels

dowel crosspiece

mounting block

lower crosspiece

end piece

Closet-door dowel rack. This compact storage unit consists of a frame and crosspieces made of 1-by-3 lumber; the pegs are ½-inch dowels and the back is ¼-inch plywood. The 1-by-3s are held together by 1½-inch No. 10 wood screws; 1-inch panel nails secure the back. All joints and dowels are fastened with wood glue.

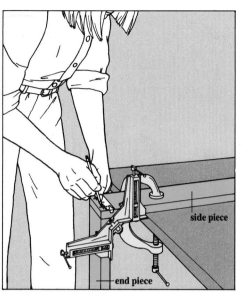

side piece

end piece

1 **Marking frame corners.** Butt a side piece and an end piece together, one end of the end piece against the face of the side piece, and secure them with a corner clamp. Use a C clamp to hold the side piece atop the worktable, then mark for two pilot holes on the side piece, ⅜ inch from the end and ¾ inch from each side. Drill counterbored pilot holes *(page 122)*, drive in screws and remove the clamps. Attach the second end piece to the other end of the side piece.

2 **Completing the frame.** Clamp the side piece to the table with the end pieces up. Add the second side piece, and clamp one corner with a corner clamp. Mark this side piece for pilot holes as you did before. Drill holes and drive in screws. Repeat for the last corner. Disassemble the frame and sand the pieces; apply glue to the ends of the end pieces, then reassemble, tightening the screws until glue squeezes out of the joints. Remove excess glue with a damp cloth.

3 **Attaching the back panel.** Lay the back panel over the edges of the frame to check fit. Remove it and run a thin bead of wood glue along the edges of the frame. Lay the back panel on the frame, aligning the edges precisely. Hammer 1-inch panel nails through the back along a line ⅜ inch from the edges, starting with three nails evenly spaced along each side. Then fill in the spaces, hammering a nail about every 8 inches. At the ends, drive nails at the center and 2 inches from each corner. ▶

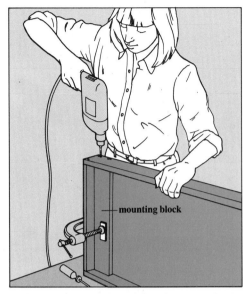

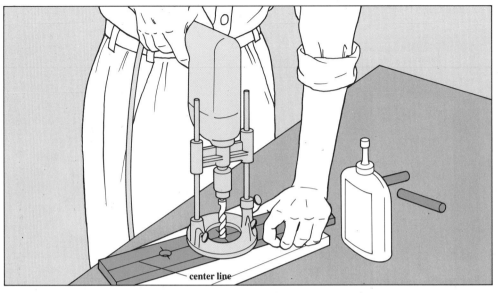

4 **Installing mounting blocks.** Spread a thin coat of glue on the back of a mounting block, and clamp the block snugly against the back and end of the frame. On the side piece, mark two pilot holes 1½ and 2½ inches from the end and ⅝ inch from the back of the frame. Drill countersunk holes at the marks, and drive screws. Repeat at the other end of the mounting block, then install the second mounting block in the same way.

5 **Drilling holes for dowels.** Draw a center line along the length of the face of each dowel block and dowel crosspiece. On the blocks, mark the center lines for dowel holes 3 inches from each end and in the center (7½ inches from the ends). On the center line of the crosspieces, mark 4½ inches from each end and in the center (8¼ inches from the ends). Set each marked piece on a scrap of wood; drill dowel holes through the piece at the marks, using a ½-inch wood bit and a drill guide.

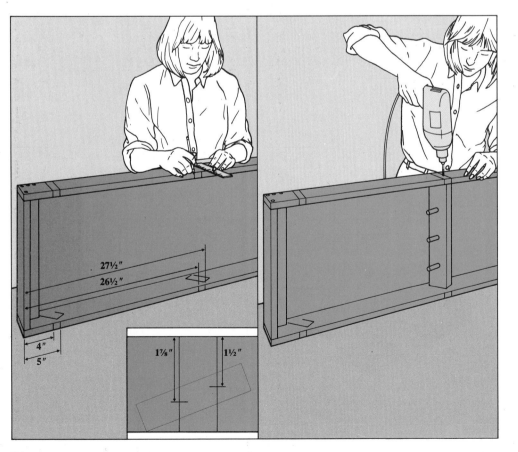

9 **Making dowel-block pilot holes.** Make marks along each side of the frame 4 inches, 5 inches, 26½ inches and 27½ inches from the top (*far left*). Use a combination square to draw a line across the outside of the side piece at each mark. On the lines at 4 and 26½ inches, make a mark 1⅞ inches from the front edge of the frame (*inset*). On the lines at 5 and 27½ inches, mark 1½ inches from the front edge of the frame.

Hold the lower dowel block in place, using the outlines you traced as a guide. Drill holes at the marks, through the frame and into the end of the dowel block (*near left*). Drive screws into the holes. Turn the frame over and attach the other end of the block. Install the upper block similarly. Mark the dowel blocks and remove them. Spread a thin coat of glue within the outlines on the inside of the frame, replace the dowel blocks and reinsert the screws.

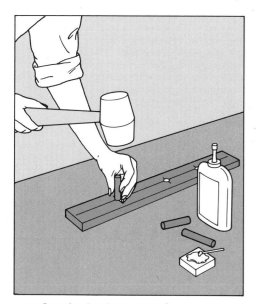

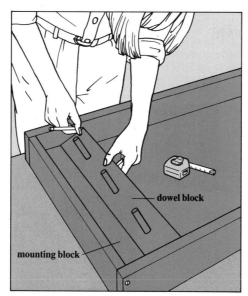

dowel block

mounting block

28 "   ¾ "

6 **Inserting dowels into holes.** Squeeze a small pool of wood glue onto a piece of scrap wood or paper. Dip a small stick into the glue, and use it to coat the inside of a dowel hole. Push a dowel into the hole, or tap it in with a wood mallet, until its end stops flush with the other side of the board. Repeat for each dowel; wipe off excess glue.

7 **Positioning the upper dowel block.** Wedge the back edge of one dowel block against the bottom of the upper mounting block. Move the outer corners of the dowel block ¾ inch below the edges of the frame and, holding the dowel block in this position, trace around both ends on the inside of the frame. Remove the dowel block.

8 **Positioning the lower dowel block.** Make a mark on the front edge of each side piece, 28 inches from the top of the frame. At each mark, measure down the inside of the frame ¾ inch, and make another mark. Place the second dowel block inside the frame, its back edge against the back panel of the frame, and its front corners aligned with the marks. Trace around both ends on the inside of the frame; remove the dowel block.

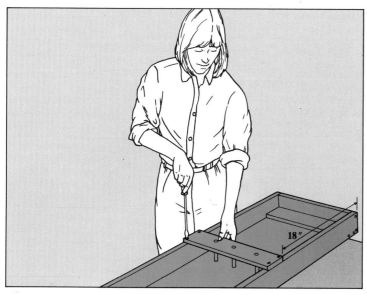

18 "

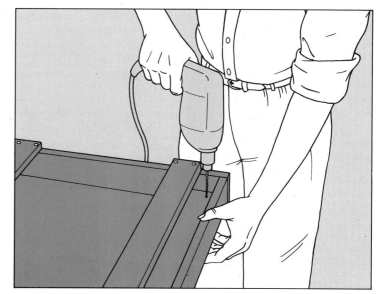

10 **Attaching the crosspieces.** Make marks 18 inches from the bottom along the front edge of each side piece. Align the lower edge of the dowel crosspiece with the marks, the dowels facing in, and use a C clamp to secure it at one edge. At the opposite edge, mark for two holes ⅜ inch from the end and ¾ inch from each side. Drill counterbored holes at the marks and drive the screws. Remove the C clamp from the other edge of the crosspiece, drill holes and drive screws. To attach the lower crosspiece, make marks 2 inches from the bottom of each side piece; position the lower edge of the crosspiece at the marks and attach it as above. Disassemble the crosspieces and sand them; then glue them and reassemble.

11 **Drilling holes for mounting.** Mark two pilot-hole positions on each mounting block: If the rack will be mounted on a hollow-core door, mark near the center line of the mounting block, 2 inches from each end. If it is a frame-and-panel door, position the marks so that the screws will enter the frame of the door. Use a ¼-inch bit to drill pilot holes at each mark.

To mount the rack, have a helper hold it in position while you lightly tap an eightpenny nail through each mounting hole, marking the surface of the door. Drill holes at the marks for the mounting screws or toggle bolts *(page 125),* then have your helper hold the rack as you drive the screws or bolts through it into the door.

An angled rack for shoes

This simple wood rack can help you transform a jumble on the closet floor into a tidy array of paired shoes, easy to see and reach. The angled shelf tucks against the back wall of the closet; a low cleat across the back of the shelf holds heels of any height. And by cutting the shelf for a close fit, you can make the rack look as though it were built into the closet.

This design requires only two pieces of wood: a 1-by-12 board, at least 8 inches longer than the width of the closet, that provides both the shelf and its two rear supports; and a strip of ¾-inch quarter-round molding, as long as the width of the closet, to form the heel cleat.

Four No. 10 wood screws 1½ inches long join the supports to the bottom of the shelf; the heel cleat is attached with several 1¼-inch finishing nails. All of the joints are also reinforced with carpenter's wood glue.

A coat of varnish or enamel imparts a finished look and makes the rack easier to wipe clean. Before applying a finish, fill all of the nail and screw holes with wood putty. Using a putty knife, form mounds of putty over the holes: The putty will shrink as it dries. Let the putty dry overnight before sanding it; the surface may feel dry to the touch within an hour or so, but the putty underneath is slow to harden. Sand the putty smooth. If the holes then look depressed, fill and sand them again. Sand the edges of the shelf, then brush on the finish according to the manufacturer's instructions.

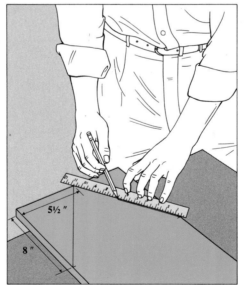

1 Making shelf supports. Measure along one end of the 1-by-12 board, making a mark 5½ inches from one corner. Measure from the same corner down the edge of the board, making a mark 8 inches from the corner. Use a straightedge to draw a line connecting the two marks. Do the same at the other corner. Clamp the board to the worktable, and cut along each line with a crosscut saw, starting from the edges of the board and cutting toward the end.

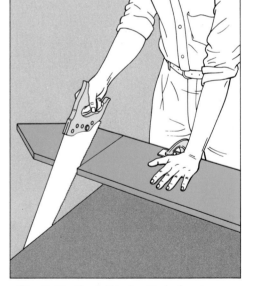

2 Cutting the shelf to size. Beginning at the uncut end of the board, measure the length needed for the shelf. This should be ¼ inch less than the width of the closet, measured between the thickest parts of the baseboard moldings. Mark this length on each edge of the board and use a straightedge to draw a line connecting the marks. Clamp the board to the table, and cut along the line with a crosscut saw.

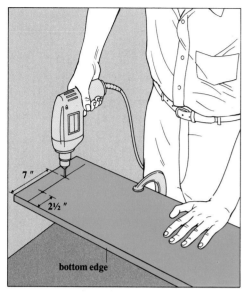

3 **Drilling holes in the shelf.** Draw lines on the front face of the shelf 2 inches from each end. Along each line, mark for screw holes 2½ inches and 7 inches from what will be the bottom edge of the shelf. Drill counterbored shank holes for No. 10 wood screws at the marks.

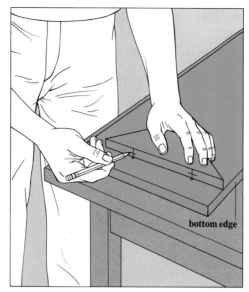

4 **Marking the pilot holes.** On the back of the shelf, align the longest edge of one support at a time with a pair of shank holes, holding the point of the support's sharpest angle even with the shelf's bottom edge. Mark each shank-hole position on the edge of the support. Draw a line across each mark at the midpoint of the support's edge.

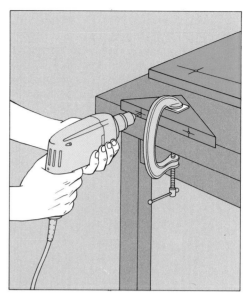

5 **Drilling the pilot holes.** Clamp the support to the worktable, using a scrap of wood to protect the support from the clamp's jaw. Drill a ¾-inch-deep pilot hole in the center of each cross, holding the drill bit at right angles to the edge of the support.

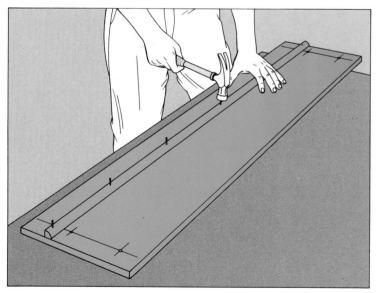

6 **Creating a heel cleat.** Cut a strip of ¾-inch quarter-round molding to the same length as the shelf. First lay the strip on the worktable with one flat side down, and drive 1¼-inch finishing nails about ½ inch into the rounded side. Locate the first and last nails about an inch from the ends, then space the rest about 10 inches apart. Draw a line on the face of the shelf, 3 inches from the top edge. Squeeze a narrow bead of wood glue ¼ inch below the line. Position the square corner of the cleat along the line, with the flat edge facing the top of the shelf, and press the cleat into the glue. Drive the nails into the shelf (*above*); use a nail set to countersink the heads. Wipe away excess glue with a damp cloth.

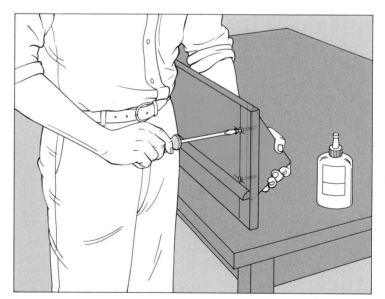

7 **Attaching the supports.** Insert 1½-inch No. 10 wood screws through the pilot holes at one end of the shelf. Spread a thin coat of glue on the pilot-hole edge of a shelf support. Stand the shelf on its top edge under one arm and hold the support against the back of the shelf, aligning the pilot holes with the tips of the screws. Drive the screws into the support. Attach the second support in the same way.

Dividing the space for systematic storage

Inside an old-fashioned clothes closet often lurks not a skeleton but a floor-to-ceiling eyesore: a mountain of shoes, clothes, hats and personal impedimenta. But a closet divider such as the one shown below can be designed to organize this jumble with neat, accessible storage tailored to a modern wardrobe.

The single high clothes rod on the left-hand side of this divider takes long garments — here, dresses and robes. The double-decker rods at the right-hand side are for short pieces of apparel, such as jackets and shirts. The central shelves accommodate shoes and slippers as well as sweaters, casual shirts and hats; vinyl-coated wire drawers hold stockings and underwear. The shelf at the left-hand side is filled with handbags.

The divider built here fits a closet 85 inches high, 86 inches wide and 24 inches deep. But it is readily adaptable, with a few provisos. Because many rooms are not perfectly square, measure your closet's height, width and depth in at least two locations, and base your plans on the smaller figures. If the central shelf unit is to include ready-made baskets, the unit's width must match theirs — from 12 to 21 inches. In any case, for ease of installation, the central unit should not be more than 30 inches wide. Shelves at the sides should not exceed 3 feet; if they do, fasten a wood cleat along the closet's back wall to keep them from sagging.

The basic materials are standard lumberyard items. The shelves and uprights are cut from 4-by-8-foot sheets of ¾-inch plywood; for accuracy, saw sheets of this size on a table saw *(pages 120-121)* — or have a lumberyard or millwork saw them for you. The divider's fittings, such as clothes rods and colorful wire baskets, are available at lumberyards, department stores or closet specialty shops.

To build the divider, a basic carpenter's kit — power drill, saber saw, steel square, miter box and such — is supplemented by a few inexpensive specialized tools. To drive this project's dozens of screws, use a power drill equipped with a screwdriver bit; a No. 2 Phillips™ bit and matching screws are best, because a Phillips bit seldom strips a screw's head.

To fit the unit to a closet's baseboard *(Step 6)*, use a dime-store compass or a pair of draftsman's dividers to mark on the unit the exact curve of the baseboard. To support the clothes rods, wood cleats are drilled with a 1½-inch hole saw — a toothed steel cylinder mounted on a central mandrel, whose short twist bit bores ahead of the saw and guides it *(Step 10)*. And to install the cleats in confined spaces, you will need a torpedo level *(Step 11)*, a cousin of a carpenter's level.

The actual work of assembling and installing the divider is simple. Once the closet's old fittings are removed *(page 19, Steps 1-2)*, the only difficulty is the new unit's considerable size. If your worktable is not long enough to accommodate it, place the unit on two sawhorses or on the floor. And enlist a helper to maneuver the unit into the closet.

Materials List

Plywood	1½ sheets of ¾″ AA-quality fir plywood, cut into:
	2 panels, 15″ wide, cut to fit your closet's height; 6 shelves, 15″ x 22″; 1 shelf, 12″ x 22″; 1 shelf, 12″ deep, cut to fit your closet *(Step 14)*
Lumber	1 clear pine 1 x 3 cleat, 22″ long 2 clear pine 1 x 6s, 8′ long, cut into:
	1 cleat, 15″ long; 2 cleats, 12″ long; 3 cleats, 22″ long 1⅜″-diameter birch clothes rod, cut to fit your closet 2 pieces ¾″ x ⅜″ parting bead, 8′ long
Baskets	3 vinyl-coated wire baskets, 3⅜″ x 13″ x 21″, with glides and screws
Wood Screws	21 No. 10 flat-head screws, 1½″ long; 16 No. 10 flat-head screws, 3″ long; 12 No. 6 flat-head screws, 1¼″ long
Nails	12 sixpenny finishing nails

A closet divider. This unit's plywood uprights — notched to give more space for maneuvering objects in front of the top shelves — carry between them glides for a bank of wire baskets with plywood shelves above and below it. The uprights are cut to fit around the closet's baseboard, toenailed to the floor and nailed to a wood mounting cleat that is screwed to the back wall's studs. Each clothes rod rests in holes drilled through cleats that are screwed to the side walls and the uprights. To simplify painting, wood strips are nailed and glued over all exposed plywood edges.

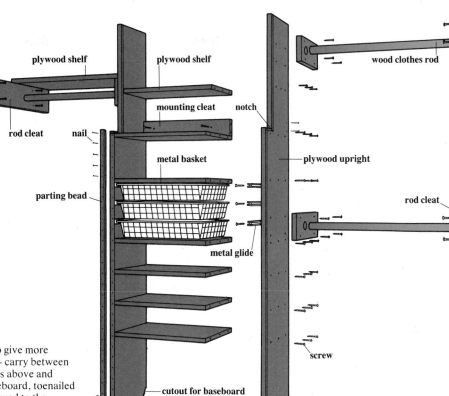

1 **Notching the uprights.** Set a 15-by-85-inch piece of ¾-inch plywood flat on a large worktable or on two sawhorses. Using a steel tape, mark one of the plywood's side edges 23 inches from an end, then use a steel square to pencil a line across the panel at the mark. Measure 3 inches from one side of the panel and draw a second line perpendicular to the first, thus outlining a narrow rectangle at one corner of the plywood. Place strips of masking tape just beyond the rectangle's top and side edges to keep the plywood from splintering; cut inside the tape with a saber saw. Smooth the cut edges with a sanding block fitted with medium (100-grit) sandpaper. Mark and cut a second piece of plywood.

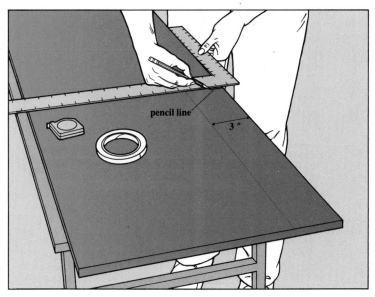

2 **Marking shelf positions.** Using a steel tape, mark the bottom of each shelf on the unnotched edge of one plywood upright, placing tick marks 18, 24, 30, 36, 48, 57 and 66 inches from the panel's unnotched end. At each mark, pencil a right-angled line across the upright's face with a steel square, then label the marked face IN. Turn the upright onto its other face. Setting the square across the upright ⅜ inch above each edge mark, indicate locations for screw holes in the panel's center and 2 inches from each edge. Mark the second upright as a mirror image of the first, so that when the uprights are installed, with their notches facing forward, the IN marks will face each other. ▶

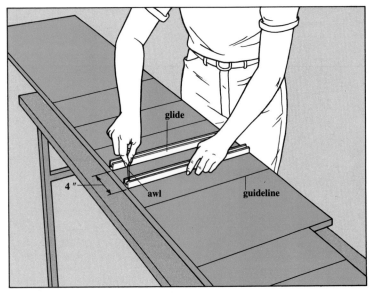

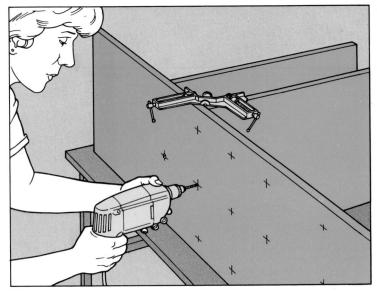

3 Installing the glides. Use a steel square to mark lines across each upright's inner face 40, 44 and 48 inches from the upright's unnotched end. Set a metal glide beneath each line. Press and twist an awl in the plywood through each glide's screw holes, then fasten the glide with the screws supplied by the manufacturer.

4 Attaching the shelves. Hold an upright on edge, with its notch facing up. Place a 15-by-22-inch shelf on edge at a right angle to the upright's inner side, and set the shelf's end atop the upright's 18-inch line. Secure the resulting joint with a corner clamp. At the three marks on the upright's outer face, drill countersunk shank and pilot holes for 1½-inch No. 10 wood screws through the upright into the shelf's end. Drive screws loosely into the holes, and remove the corner clamp. Fasten shelves atop the upright's other lines in the same way, then screw each shelf's free end loosely to the other upright.

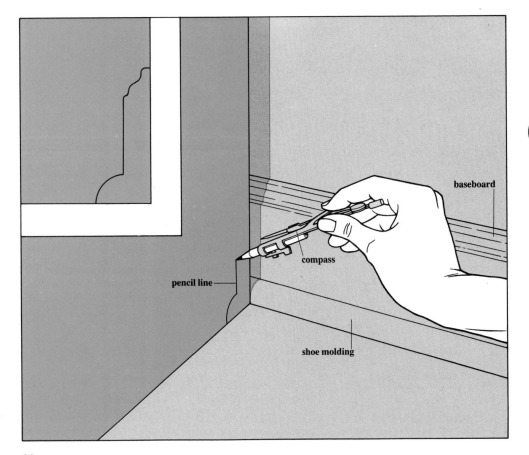

6 Scribing for the baseboard. Hold a pair of dividers or, as here, a dime-store compass horizontal above the baseboard beside one upright. Set the metal leg's point against the wall and adjust the opposite leg until its pencil lead rests against the upright's edge. Then use the compass or dividers to mark the baseboard's exact silhouette on the plywood (inset): While keeping the legs horizontal and holding the pencil point against the upright, set the metal point on the floor against the shoe molding, and draw it upward along the molding and baseboard to the wall.

Scribe the other upright similarly, then reverse the procedure in Step 5 to remove the unit from the closet. Cut along the marked silhouette on each upright with a saber saw and smooth the cut edges with medium (100-grit) sandpaper.

5 **Emplacing the unit.** Unscrew one upright, and set it aside. With a helper, tilt the rest of the unit, and slide it through the closet door. Set the upright's rear bottom corner against the closet's back baseboard and put the upright in a vertical position. Set the second upright against the baseboard in the same way; fasten it to the free end of each shelf with one temporary screw.

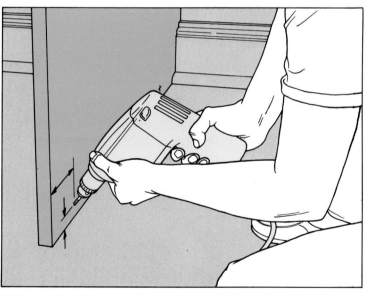

7 **Toenailing the uprights.** Put the unit into the closet *(Step 5)*, this time permanently fastening the pieces with snugly tightened screws. Slide the unit sideways to its desired position, measuring from each side wall to the unit about 6 inches above the floor. Mark the outer face of each upright for pilot holes 3 inches from each edge, placing the marks an inch above the floor. Set a 3/32-inch twist bit on each mark, angling the drill down at about 60° so the hole will not break through the upright's other side. Holding the drill very firmly to prevent it from skipping to the left, drill down to the floor. Use a claw hammer to drive a sixpenny finishing nail into each hole; countersink the nailheads with a nail set.

8 **Plumbing the unit.** Hold a carpenter's level vertical against one upright. If the upright is not plumb, force the unit's top sideways by pushing it with your hands; to move uprights that are tightly wedged against the ceiling, hold a 2-by-4 block flat against an upright, and tap the block with a hammer. When the upright is plumb, faintly mark the position of its outer face on the closet's back wall. ▶

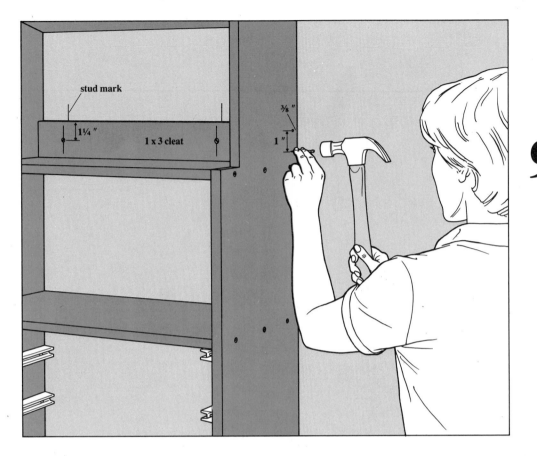

stud mark

1¼ ″

1 x 3 cleat

⅜ ″

1 ″

9 **Installing the cleat.** Mark the back wall's stud locations *(page 124)* just above the shelf that adjoins the notches in the uprights. Set the cleat, a 22-inch 1-by-3, on edge on the shelf; press it against the wall, and transfer the stud lines to the cleat. On each line, drill a countersunk shank hole for a 3-inch No. 10 wood screw in the cleat's center, then through these holes drill pilot holes in the studs. Screw the cleat to the wall.

Hammer two sixpenny finishing nails through each upright into the ends of the cleat, placing the nails ⅜ inch from the upright's edge and 1 inch apart. Countersink the nailheads with a nail set.

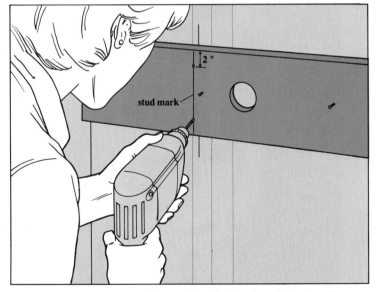

2 ″

stud mark

12 **Securing the cleats.** Over each marked stud, mark the cleats for screw holes 2 inches from the top and bottom edges. At each mark, drill countersunk shank and pilot holes for 3-inch No. 10 wood screws through the cleat into the stud; screw the cleats to the studs. Remove the temporary nails with the claw hammer.

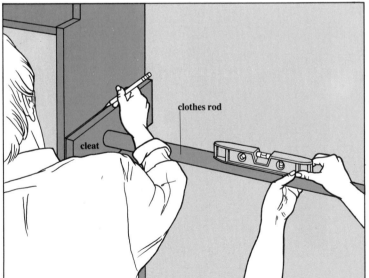

clothes rod

cleat

13 **Leveling a rod.** Set a clothes rod's end in the hole in one of the already mounted cleats, and slide the hole in an unmounted cleat over the rod's other end. Use a 12-inch cleat for a rod located above the upright's notch, a 15-inch cleat for a rod located below. Have a helper hold a torpedo level atop the rod while you hold the free cleat against the upright and adjust its height until the rod is level. Then mark the cleat's top on the upright just above the rod. With the rod still in place, level the free cleat *(Step 11)* and permanently fasten it to the upright with four 1¼-inch No. 6 wood screws, placed 2 inches from each corner of the cleat.

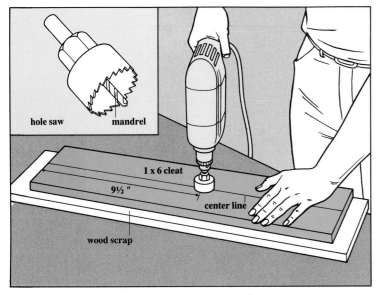

hole saw   mandrel

1 x 6 cleat

9½"

center line

wood scrap

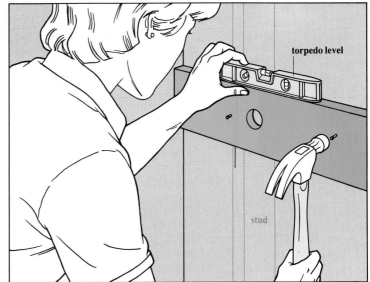

torpedo level

stud

10 **Drilling a cleat.** Mark a hole on the center line of a 1-by-6 cleat 9½ inches from one of the cleat's ends. Place the cleat atop a scrap of wood on a worktable. Set the mandrel of a 1½-inch hole saw (*inset*) on the mark, hold the cleat down firmly and drill half-way through the cleat. Turn over the cleat, slide the mandrel into its old pilot hole and finish drilling the larger hole; then slide the resulting doughnut of wood out of the hole saw. Mark and drill the other five cleats in the same way.

11 **Leveling a wall cleat.** Mark the planned height of the side shelf's bottom (here, 72¼ inches) on the closet's side wall near the corner. Add 2 inches to the planned height of each closet rod that will not be surmounted by a shelf, and mark these dimensions (here, 44 and 82 inches) similarly on the other side wall. Near the level of each cleat mark, pencil the location of each side wall's studs. Place a 22-inch cleat flat on a side wall, with its hole near the closet's back wall. Align the cleat's top with the height mark, and drive a temporary nail below the mark; let the nail protrude for easy removal. Set a torpedo level on the cleat, level its front end and tap in a temporary nail. Then level the other two wall cleats.

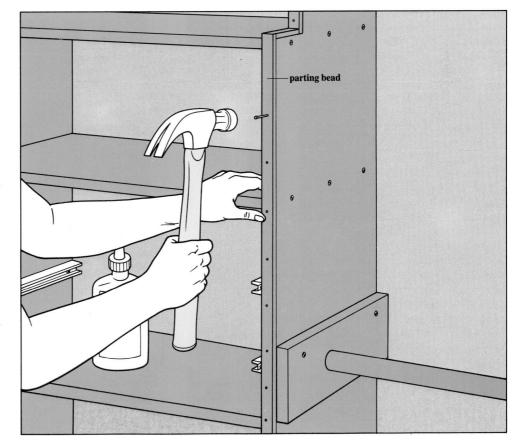

parting bead

14 **Covering plywood edges.** Cut a 12-inch-deep plywood shelf to fit between the left side wall of the closet and the adjacent upright, and set the shelf on the rod's cleats; it need not be fastened with nails or screws. Working down from the top of the closet, cover the exposed edge of one upright at a time with a strip of ¾-by-⅜-inch wood, generally known as parting bead. Cut each strip to length with a miter box and a backsaw, and apply a thin line of glue to one side; then fasten the strip to the upright's edge with 1-inch brads driven at 4-inch intervals. Cover the front edge of each shelf similarly. Countersink the brads with a nail set and wipe away excess glue with a damp rag.

Mothproofing with fragrant cedar paneling

The old-fashioned practice of lining a closet with aromatic red cedar to repel moths still makes sense. The faintly spicy fragrance that people find so appealing keeps moths away from woolens without help from camphor or chemicals. Moreover, so-called closet cedar is readily available in boards 2½ to 4½ inches wide and ⅜ inch thick that are tongued and grooved on all four edges so they can be installed snugly with a minimum of waste.

Depending on the manufacturer, cedar is sold either in cartons containing boards of a uniform 42-inch length or bundled into packages containing assorted lengths of from 10 inches to 8 feet. Whatever its packaging, it is sold by the square foot.

For a mothproof closet, the boards may be applied to the walls alone, also to the ceiling as demonstrated here, or even to the back of the door. The more complete the lining, the greater its effectiveness. To determine how much cedar you need, first measure each area and multiply the length by the width; then add these figures together and include a 10 per cent allowance for waste. Besides paneling, aromatic cedar is available in 1-by-12 and 1-by-4 lumber, providing material for shelves and for cleats to hold them.

Like any paneling, cedar can be installed horizontally or vertically. It can be put up with panel adhesive or nails.

When adhesive is used, ceiling boards can be installed parallel or perpendicular to the joists. For nailing, the boards must be set perpendicular to joists and attached with so-called blind, or hidden, nails except at the ends, where face, or exposed, nails are necessary.

To lie flat, paneling must have smooth, plumb walls behind it. If walls pass the test in Step 5, the boards can simply be cemented in place, nailed horizontally to studs or nailed vertically to a base of ⅜-inch plywood that is hung on the studs. If walls are not flat, they must be furred with 1-by-2s and plywood added for either cementing or nailing.

A caution: If you use adhesive, be wary of its toxic fumes. Set up a fan and frequently step out of the closet for fresh air while you work.

Once installed, cedar needs no maintenance. Quite the contrary: Varnish or wax would seal in its aroma. However, if the aroma fades with time, it can be refreshed by sanding the cedar lightly.

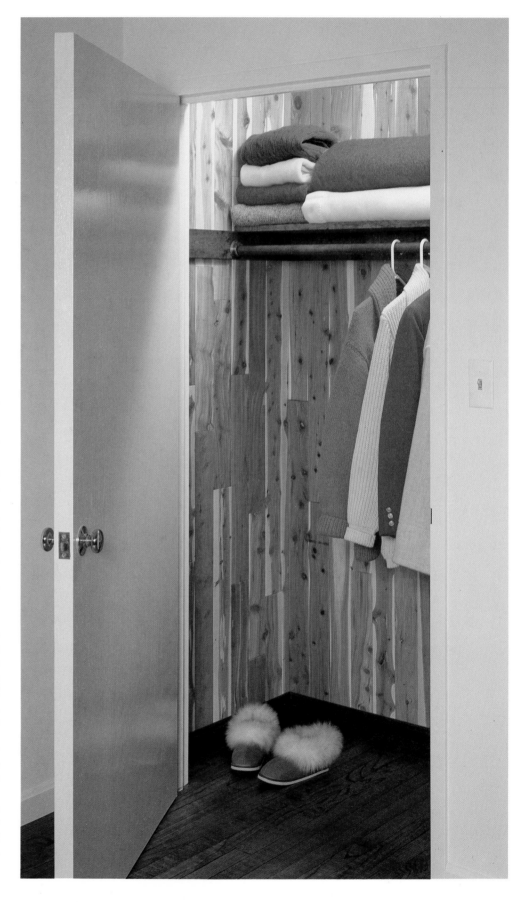

1 **Preparing the closet.** Remove the clothes rod and shelf as described on page 19. To pull out the baseboard without damaging it, first slit the paint seal between the baseboard and wall with a utility knife. Then, starting near the end of the molding at one side of the door, tap a small pry bar into the seam behind the baseboard. Insert a thin, smooth piece of wood behind the pry bar to increase your leverage. Pry the baseboard away from the wall, inserting shims — tapered wood scraps or shingles — as you proceed, until the length of baseboard is loose enough to pull away in one piece. If there is quarter-round molding in front of the baseboard, free it first — using the same techniques. If there is molding at the ceiling or corners, pry it off as well.

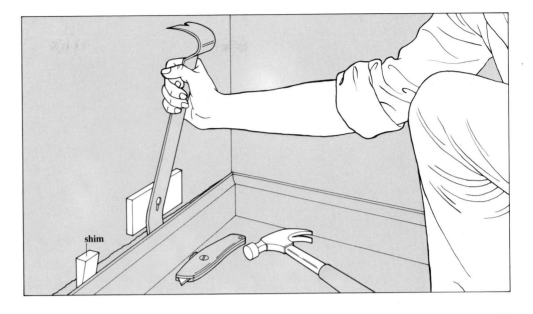

shim

nail set

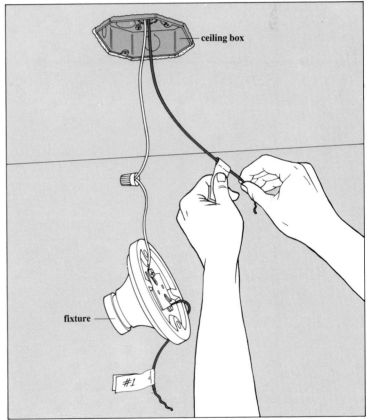

ceiling box

fixture

#1

2 **Removing the inner door casing.** On the inside of the closet, slit the paint seal between the door casing and wall with the utility knife. To avoid splitting the molding as you remove it, use a nail set and hammer at each mitered corner to carefully drive the heads of the nails — called lock nails — completely through the molding. With the pry bar and shims, free the molding in three pieces — first from each of the sides, then from above the door. Set all of the molding aside.

3 **Removing an overhead light fixture.** After switching off the power to the closet at the service panel, remove the light bulb, then the screws that hold the base of the fixture to the ceiling box. Pull the fixture down and away from the box until the wire caps that connect the various leads are visible. Twist off each wire cap in turn, marking the leads that belong together with numbers penciled onto tape to ease rewiring the fixture later. With the help of a licensed electrician, or alone if you are familiar with home wiring, lower the ceiling box ⅜ inch so its bottom edge will be flush with ceiling paneling. In most cases, you can do this just by moving the box down the side of the joist to which it is nailed. ▶

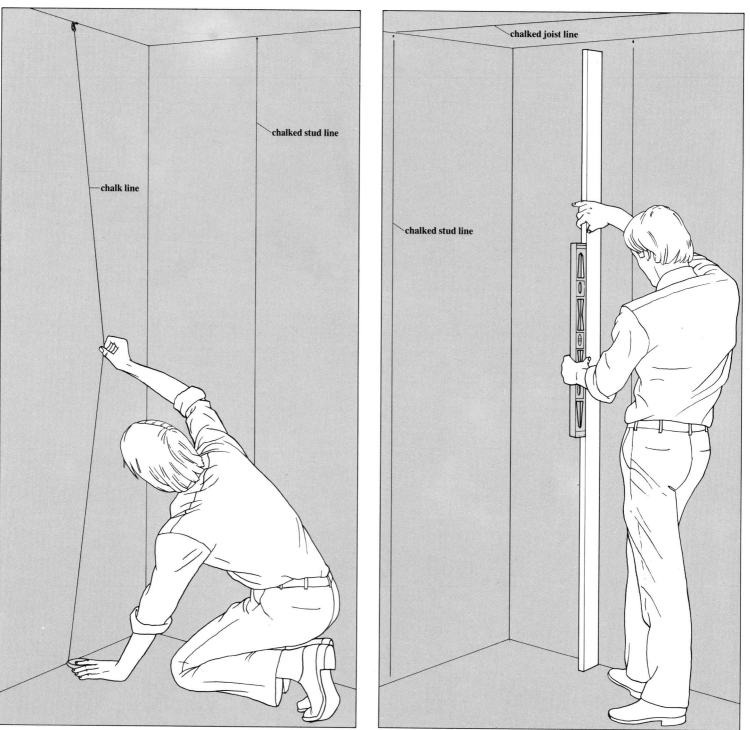

chalk line

chalked stud line

chalked joist line

chalked stud line

4 **Marking studs and joists.** Locate the top of each wall stud (*page 124*). Tap a nail into the wall near the ceiling at the center of the stud. Attach the tab of a chalk-line string to the nail and let the line hang straight. Mark where the line hits the base of the wall, hold the line taut there and pull it back slightly several feet above the floor (*above*). Release the line to snap a chalk mark along the stud. For ceiling joists, at each wall mark the center of one joist, then snap a chalk line between marks. If the next joist is 16 inches from the chalk line — a typical dimension — simply make subsequent joist lines at 16-inch intervals.

5 **Checking walls for plumb.** With a straight board roughly equivalent to the height of the walls, check the wall surfaces for juts or valleys by sliding the edge of the board across them. Next, check each wall for plumb by holding one edge of the board flush against the wall in a number of places and setting a carpenter's level on the outer edge (*above*). If any walls have juts or valleys of more than ¼ to ½ inch, or are out of plumb, correct the surface with furring strips, as described in Steps 6 through 8. Otherwise proceed to Step 9 to panel the ceiling.

6 **Truing furring strips.** Cut 1-by-2s to fit across the top and bottom of one closet wall. These will serve as furring strips, which are attached to walls to act as fastening points for new wall surfaces. Using eight-penny nails, attach the strips loosely at the corners of the wall. Hold a straight board on edge along the face of one furring strip at a time, then shim the strip out to your straight edge. Nail through the furring to secure the shim. Use your board and level to check if the two strips are plumb. If not, shim the deeper one until both are even.

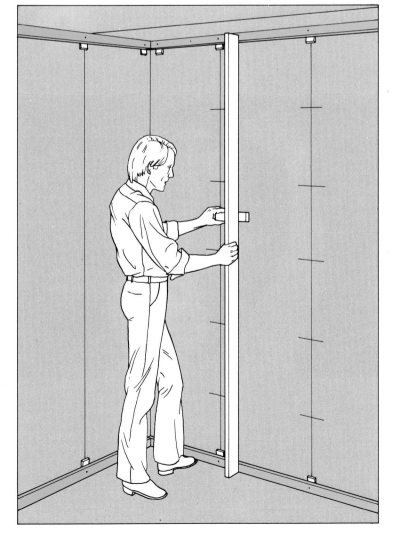

7 **Truing for intermediate strips.** On two adjacent chalked lines, mark locations for intermediate furring strips at 16-inch intervals. In front of one marked stud line, bridge a straight board across the top and bottom furring strips. Attempt to pass a 1-by-2 scrap between the board and wall at several places. If the 1-by-2 fits, nail intermediate strips to the studs; if gaps exceed $1/16$ inch, shim each middle strip out to the board.

If the 1-by-2 does not pass under the board, note the distance between the board and wall at each mark. Nail one intermediate horizontal strip where the gap is narrowest. True the strip, then use a board and level to plumb this strip with the ceiling strip by shimming the ceiling strip. Attach the remaining strips similarly.

Fur each wall in turn. On the front wall, fur around the door, abutting the jambs. ▶

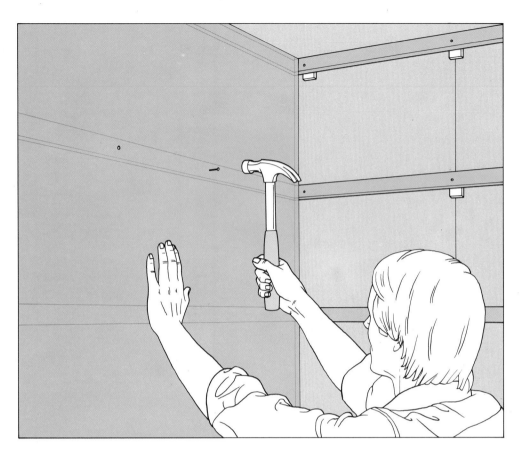

8 **Sheathing with plywood.** To be certain that all abutting ends of the paneling will be supported from behind, measure each wall in turn and cut a piece of 5/16-inch CD plywood to fit it exactly. Nail the sheet in place by driving threepenny nails into the furring strips at 1-foot intervals.

If the height of a wall necessitates more than one plywood sheet, mount the lower one horizontally. Cut the sheet so its upper edge will be centered on a furring strip, nail it, then rest the upper sheet on the edge of the lower one while nailing it in place.

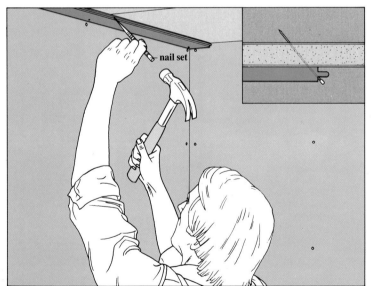

nail set

11 **Nailing.** Saw off the tongue end to cut the board to fit from wall to wall, perpendicular to the joists. Or piece boards together for the requisite length. Place the grooved or ripped side tight against the corner. If one end of the closet is narrower, set the board flush in that corner and up to 3/8 inch from the side wall at the opposite corner — to begin "fanning" the strips to absorb excess space. Tap two red-topped panel nails through the board's face 1 inch from the side wall, the first near the corner, the second at the nearest joist. Then, with a nail set, blind-nail the board by tapping a threepenny finishing nail at a 45° angle into the joist through the base of the tongue *(inset)*. Repeat at each joist and the other corner.

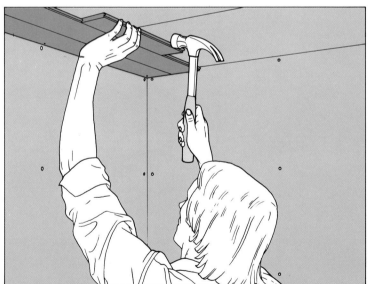

12 **Installing subsequent boards.** Insert the side groove of the next board onto the side tongue of the board you just installed. If you are using short lengths of cedar, connect the tongue and groove at the ends of the boards. If necessary, have a helper hold the boards in position. To be certain that the boards are correctly seated, use a 1-foot piece of cedar as a hammering block. Slip the groove of the hammering block over the tongue of the newly added board and gently tap the edge of the block with a hammer until the joint is tight. Leave about 1/16 inch of the tongue exposed between the boards at the end you are fanning. Blind-nail the tongue edge at every joist.

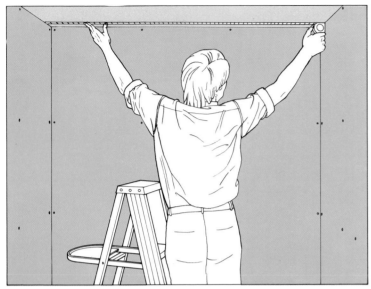

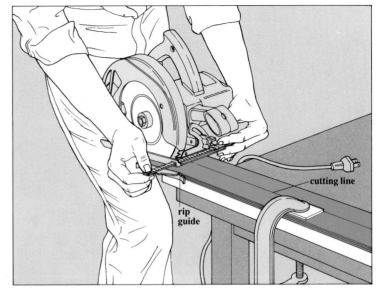

9 **Computing ceiling paneling.** First, measure the ceiling at right angles to the joists to determine how many boards you need to piece together to obtain this length for each strip. If you will need to cut a board, plan to saw off the tongue end. Then to ensure that the final strip on the ceiling will not be overly narrow, measure the ceiling parallel to the joists *(above)* at both ends. Divide the smaller measurement by the width of a board. If the remainder is less than half a board wide, add that amount to the full width of a board and divide by 2; then saw both the first and last strips of boards lengthwise — a process known as ripping *(Step 10)* — to make them the necessary width.

10 **Ripping a board to width.** Measuring from the grooved side, make several ticks on the underside of a board to mark the width required; connect the ticks with a cutting line as long as the board. Clamp the board to a worktable, with the groove outward. Use a scrap of the same length under it to protect the table; do not let the scrap extend beyond the groove. With the saw unplugged, hold its base plate on the end of the board and align the inner edge of a combination-type blade on the waste side of the cutting line. Set up a straightedge guide *(page 119)*, or adjust a rip guide *(above)* on the edge of the board to the proper distance and tighten the nut to lock the guide. Plug in the saw, and rip the board along the line.

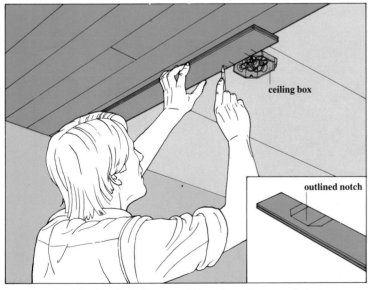

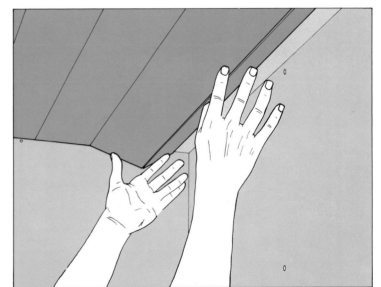

13 **Notching for a light fixture.** Add boards until you reach the ceiling box. Position the board that will cross it, and make tick marks on the underside of the tongue to indicate where the board will meet the sides of the box. Then measure the depth for the notch from the last installed board to the near edge of the ceiling box; transfer this measure onto the underside of the board. Use the ticks as a guide for drawing a rough outline of the part of the box that will be covered by the board *(inset)*; cut out the notch with a jigsaw. Install the board, then measure and notch the next board similarly.

14 **Inserting the final boards.** Set the next-to-last strip in place, but do not nail it. Measure to recheck the width of the final strip, then rip the boards if necessary — following the technique in Step 10, but cutting off the tongue side. Pull the tongue side of the next-to-last strip slightly away from the ceiling, and set the groove of the final strip over it. With the ripped strip angled upward, push both strips against the ceiling, forcing the joint shut. Face-nail both boards at every joist with panel nails.

With the power off, replace the ceiling fixture by first twisting the wires together as marked and tightening a wire cap onto each pair. Push up the wires, and screw the fixture into place. ▶

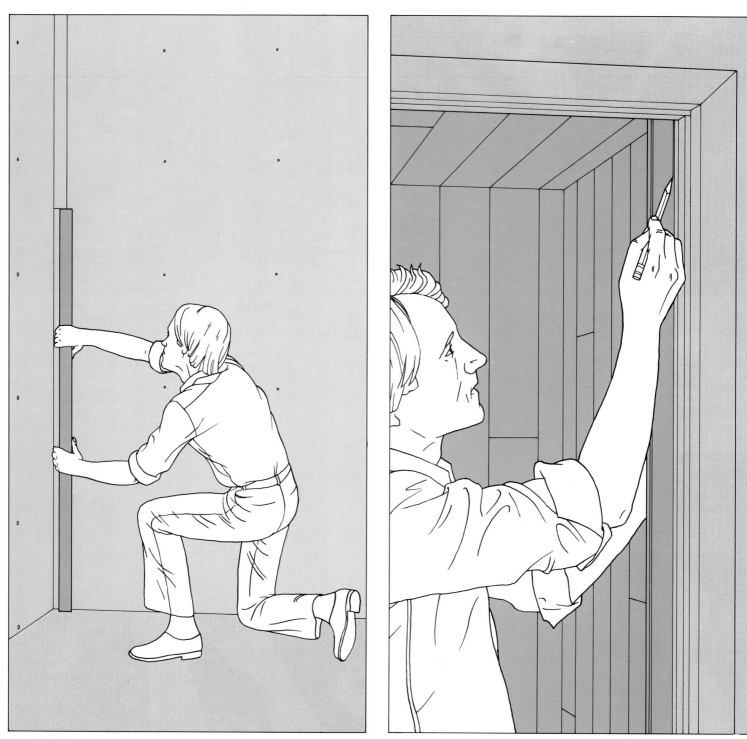

15 **Fitting boards to the walls.** Measure the back wall to calculate the length and width of the first board, or boards, as explained in Step 9; then rip, cut and nail boards as described in Steps 10, 11 and 12. To avoid creating continuous horizontal lines across the wall, select boards so that short and long ones alternate at the top and bottom of each strip. Measure and rip the last boards for the wall as described in Step 14. Panel the side walls in similar fashion.

16 **Marking the door opening.** Work from one corner of the front wall until a board overlaps the door opening. On the rear of the board, mark where it crosses the edges of the furring strips above and beside the doorjamb. Use a crosscut saw to cut the board by hand along the line marking the top of the door; use a power saw to make the vertical cut *(Step 10)*. Face-nail the board in place. Cut and nail short boards to fit the area above the door. Then fit a board to the other side of the door and complete paneling the wall.

17 **Nailing jamb extensions.** Measure the combined thicknesses of the furring strips, plywood and cedar at the top and sides of the door. From 1-by-2s or from 1-by-4s ripped to the necessary width, cut jamb extensions. Clamp one extension at a time on edge over sawhorses or over scrap wood on a worktable. Use a power drill with a ⅛-inch twist bit to bore straight through the extension at 12-inch intervals. Drive eightpenny common nails through the holes to nail the pieces to the existing jambs.

Reattach the door casing, nailing it into place with fourpenny finishing nails. Lock-nail the corners by driving the nails straight down through the top molding into the side molding.

18 **Leveling shelf cleats.** Cut a 1-by-4 cleat to fit the closet's rear wall. Determine the proper height for the shelf top, subtract ¾ inch for the board itself and mark this height at one side of the rear wall. Hold the cleat flush against the wall at your mark, and anchor it at one end with a sixpenny finishing nail. Set the level on the cleat; hold the board level while scribing the wall at the other end. Nail the cleat at the other end and at 12-inch intervals between.

19 **Truing the cleats.** Cut, level and install the side cleats, aligning them with the rear cleat. Hold your level at an angle from the back cleat to the front of each side cleat to check for level; if necessary, tap the side cleat very lightly with a hammer and scrap of wood to correct the level. Cut a shelf from 1-by-12 stock and set it in place. Install a clothes rod, using wood sockets *(page 21)* to hold it.

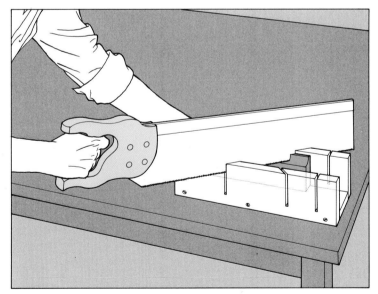

20 **Reattaching the baseboards.** Starting with the section at one side of the door, measure the new length for each of the baseboard sections you removed in Step 1. Use a backsaw and miter box to cut the square end that abuts the door casing; preserve the existing 45° angle for the corner. Nail this section by tapping in fourpenny finishing nails, at a downward 45° angle, from a point halfway up the baseboard. With subsequent baseboard sections, cut a new 45° angle at one end *(above),* preserving the angle at the other end. Work in this same manner for each wall, moving in one direction around the closet to the opposite side of the door.

41

Stretching space with racks

The term "rack" is believed to have descended from the old Dutch *recken,* meaning to stretch or reach — an appropriate origin for the word applied to devices that stretch storage space by holding things within reach but out of the way. Broadly speaking, racks are frameworks on or in which objects are stored. A rack can be a handsome cart hung with laundry bags *(pages 62-71)* or a neat panel of pegs for hanging raincoats and umbrellas *(pages 46-47).* Varied materials and types of construction give different racks individual styles expressly suited to their functions and settings. Ready-made vinyl-coated metal grids provide workaday hooks and hangers for closets and cupboards, whereas the plywood hall tree on pages 48-51 is an elegant rack you can build for yourself.

There are jobs and places, too, for rough-and-ready racks like the ones on this and the next three pages. They provide orderly storage for such items as tools, lumber and bicycles in garage or basement — areas where the joists and studs to which you attach the racks are usually exposed. To locate concealed studs, see page 124.

Most of these racks are made of construction-grade lumber — even scrap lumber will do if it is integral. When buying a board, sight along its length to make sure it is straight; warping signals weakness and would distort joints.

Another useful and relatively inexpensive material for simple racks is pegboard — hardboard checkered with regularly spaced holes for a wide variety of slip-in metal hooks and brackets. Pegboard is readily available in sheets of 2 by 4 feet and 4 by 8 feet, and in thicknesses of ⅛ inch and, for hanging heavier objects, ¼ inch. Because dampness can make the compressed fibers swell and warp, buy Class 1 tempered hardboard pegboard; then prime it, paint it and mount it where it is not directly exposed to weather.

With both materials, use screws or bolts to hold racks together and to fix them securely in place. Prepare for either kind of fastener by drilling holes *(page 122).*

A Screwdriver Caddy

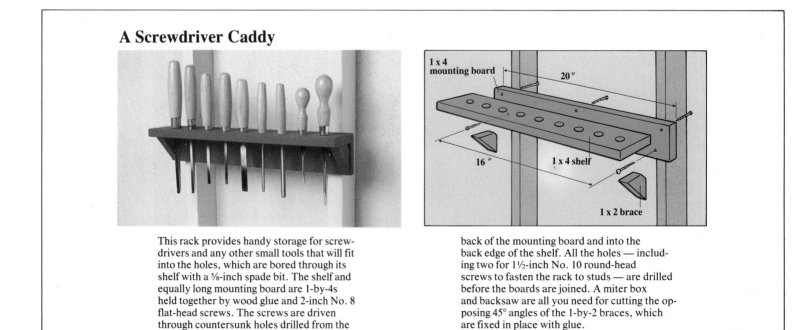

This rack provides handy storage for screwdrivers and any other small tools that will fit into the holes, which are bored through its shelf with a ⅝-inch spade bit. The shelf and equally long mounting board are 1-by-4s held together by wood glue and 2-inch No. 8 flat-head screws. The screws are driven through countersunk holes drilled from the back of the mounting board and into the back edge of the shelf. All the holes — including two for 1½-inch No. 10 round-head screws to fasten the rack to studs — are drilled before the boards are joined. A miter box and backsaw are all you need for cutting the opposing 45° angles of the 1-by-2 braces, which are fixed in place with glue.

A Gardener's Organizer

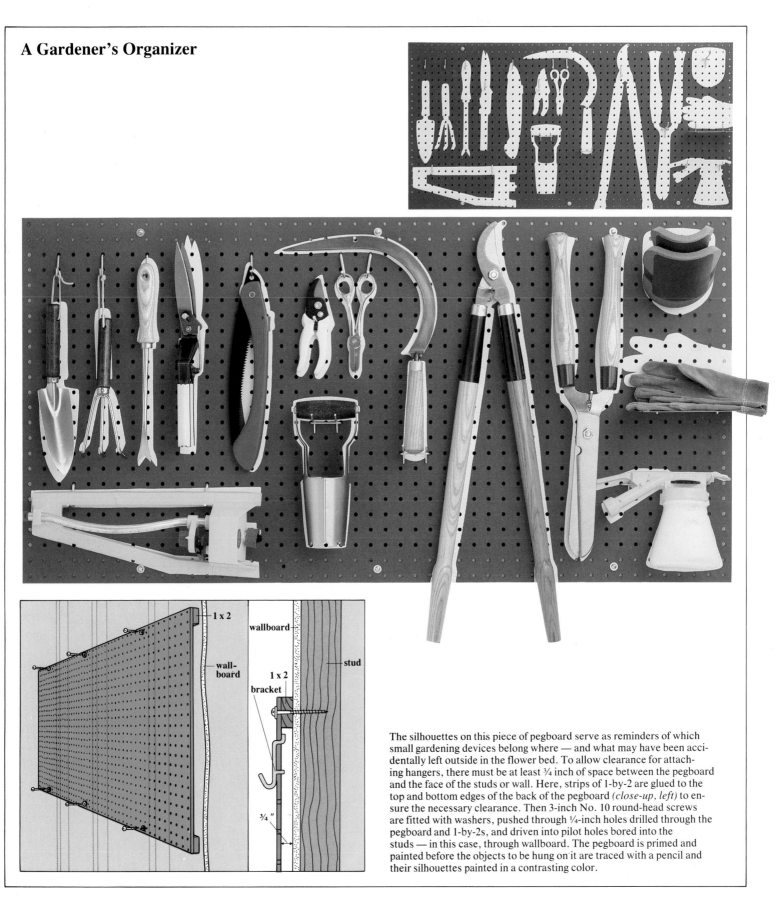

The silhouettes on this piece of pegboard serve as reminders of which small gardening devices belong where — and what may have been accidentally left outside in the flower bed. To allow clearance for attaching hangers, there must be at least ¾ inch of space between the pegboard and the face of the studs or wall. Here, strips of 1-by-2 are glued to the top and bottom edges of the back of the pegboard *(close-up, left)* to ensure the necessary clearance. Then 3-inch No. 10 round-head screws are fitted with washers, pushed through ¼-inch holes drilled through the pegboard and 1-by-2s, and driven into pilot holes bored into the studs — in this case, through wallboard. The pegboard is primed and painted before the objects to be hung on it are traced with a pencil and their silhouettes painted in a contrasting color.

Overhead Storage

 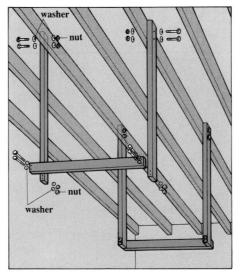 

Two U-shaped assemblies of construction-grade 2-by-3s, when hung from joists in the garage or basement, hold lumber, screen doors or other large objects up and out of the way. The length of the vertical pieces is determined by whether there is to be walk-under headroom or only clearance for a parked car. The rack works best if oriented to hold objects at right angles to the garage door; this way, long objects can be carried in and slipped directly up onto the rack.

The version at left and center, above, suits garages where joists are perpendicular to the door. For this rack, the crossbars equal the distance across three joists, plus 3 inches for the thickness of two vertical pieces. Measure from one end of the joists to mark the placement of vertical pieces; here, they are 4 feet apart. All holes are drilled with a ¼-inch twist bit, those in each overlapping piece being used to mark hole positions on the next piece or the joist. Secure the vertical pieces to the joists with 3½-inch machine bolts ¼ inch in diameter, fitted with nuts and washers as shown. Then attach the crossbars with 4½-inch bolts.

The version at right, above, suits garages where joists parallel the garage door. The crossbars should not be longer than 3 feet. Because the 2-by-3s meet face to face instead of face to edge, they can be fixed with machine bolts only 3½ inches long.

A Bicycle Holder

Two 2-by-4s braced by a 2-by-2 mitered at a 45° angle at both ends form each arm of this rack; V-shaped grooves spaced to hold a pair of adult-sized bicycles are sawed into the horizontal 2-by-4s, and felt strips are glued on to protect the bicycle paintwork. The arms are joined to the vertical supports with wood glue and 3-inch No. 10 screws driven into counterbored holes. The diagonal braces are affixed with glue and counterbored 2½-inch No. 10 screws. Use a carpenter's level to align the units. Mount them with 3-inch lag bolts, ¼ inch in diameter. The bolts are fitted with washers, pushed through ¼-inch holes drilled through the supports, and driven into ³⁄₁₆-inch pilot holes in the studs.

A Yard-Tool Center

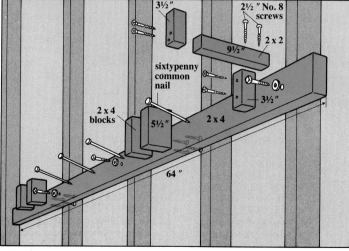

A length of 2-by-4 extending across several studs accommodates rakes, spades and the like. Blocks cut from another 2-by-4 are fixed to the first with wood glue and countersunk 2½-inch No. 8 wood screws, to form brackets sized to fit particular tools. An L-shaped arm is assembled from three pieces of 2-by-2 to hold a hose. The 2-by-4 is fastened to three studs with lag bolts, ¼ inch in diameter and 3 inches long. The bolts are fitted with washers, slipped through ¼-inch holes in the rack, and then driven into pilot holes bored in the studs with a ³⁄₁₆-inch twist bit. Finally, carpenter's spikes — sixtypenny common nails — are angled downward into the 2-by-4 to provide more hangers; to avoid splitting the wood, drive the spikes into holes predrilled with a ¹⁵⁄₆₄-inch twist bit.

An old-fashioned coatrack

Classic racks like the one below can add a warm and decorative note to an unadorned entryway. Consisting only of ⅝-inch dowels glued into angled holes in a clear pine 1-by-6, this rack is remarkably easy to build. And its design is supremely practical, with sturdy, widely spaced pegs that are long enough to hold the bulkiest coats, hats and mufflers.

Although the rack shown here is 36 inches long, the basic design can be either expanded or contracted to suit both your needs and the space available. Allow at least 7 inches between the pegs, so that their holes do not weaken the 1-by-6. And if your rack will be more than 4 feet long, add a third pair of mounting holes in the middle. In a wood-frame house, the rack commonly is fastened with brass, oval-head wood screws to the wall studs, whose centers generally are spaced 16 inches apart; 24-inch intervals are found in some newer homes. Space the mounting holes *(Step 3)* accordingly, in multiples of 16 or 24 inches; a 32-inch interval is used here. If your house does not have wood studs, or if circumstances make it impossible to hang the rack from studs, select one of the alternative fasteners discussed on page 124.

Materials for the rack must be chosen with care, because the diameter of ready-made dowels varies considerably. To ensure strong dowel joints, use a drill guide to bore an angled hole *(Step 2)* in a small 1-inch board, and use this scrap to test dowels at the lumberyard. Find a dowel that slides readily into the hole and that fits snugly, without wobbling; if necessary, a too-tight dowel can be sanded down to the proper size.

When you are gluing the dowel pegs into their holes, try to avoid smearing glue on the exposed portions of the rack, lest the glue seal patches of wood and cause an ugly, mottled finish. Wipe away visible glue immediately with a damp rag. After the glue joints have cured overnight, sand the entire rack with fine (150-grit) paper, taking special pains to sand away any glue marks that remain. Then finish the rack with stain and varnish or with alkyd paint.

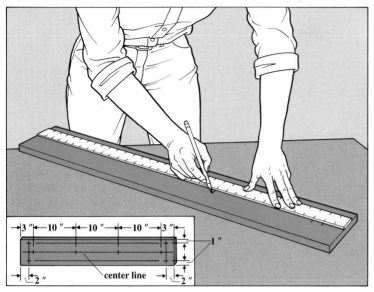

1 **Marking the holes.** Use a yardstick to draw a faint pencil line along the center of a 36-inch 1-by-6. Mark across the center line for dowel holes 3 inches from each end of the board and at 10-inch intervals between these marks. Then mark short, intersecting lines for two mounting holes at each end of the 1-by-6 (*inset*), drawing lines 2 inches from the board's ends and 1 inch from each side edge.

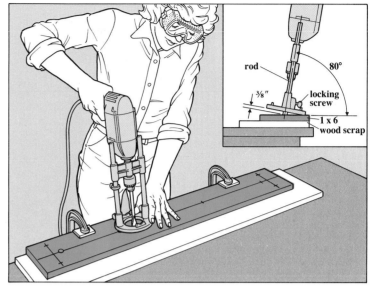

2 **Drilling dowel holes.** Center the 1-by-6 atop a long scrap of wood and secure the two pieces to the table with C clamps, using small softwood scraps to protect the board from the jaws of the clamp. Adjust the drill guide (*page 122*) to an 80° angle by sliding its rods ⅜ inch beyond the guide's base and tightening the locking screws (*inset*). Place the tip of a ⅝-inch spade bit on a dowel-hole mark, and set both of the guide's rods on the center line. Firmly hold down the near edge of the guide's base with one hand while you drill through the 1-by-6 into the scrap board below. Drill the other dowel holes in the same way.

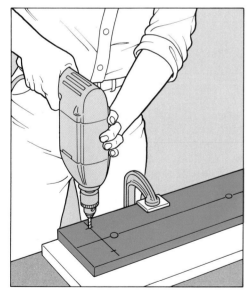

3 **Drilling mounting holes.** Hold the drill freehand, and drill 3/16-inch shank holes at the mounting-hole marks from Step 1. These holes will accommodate brass No. 10 oval-head wood screws or other appropriate fasteners (*page 124-125*).

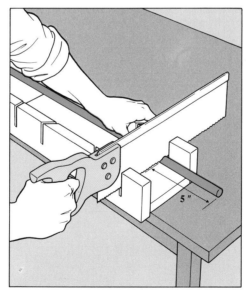

4 **Cutting the pegs.** Mark a ⅝-inch dowel 5 inches from one end, hold the dowel against the back of a miter box and use a backsaw to cut the dowel at the mark. Cut three more pegs similarly, then round one end of each peg with medium (100-grit) sandpaper.

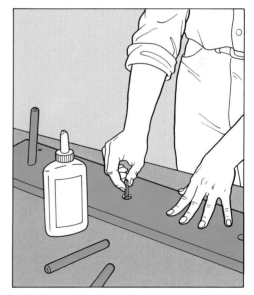

5 **Gluing the pegs.** Squeeze glue onto a splinter or a wooden matchstick, and swab the glue inside a dowel hole. Slide a peg into the hole, and wipe away excess glue with a damp rag. Install the remaining pegs similarly. Let the glue set overnight. Sand the rack with fine (150-grit) paper. Then finish it with paint or varnish.

An elegant hall tree

orm follows function wonderfully well in this graceful hall tree for coats and hats; what is more, the elegant simplicity and perfect symmetry of its design make it easy to build. The twelve pieces comprise four identical sets of hooks, legs and vertical supports. These are assembled with glue and wood screws one set at a time, and then two sets are joined to form halves; finally, the halves are glued and screwed together to produce the finished hall tree.

Reproducing this hall tree calls for making leg and hook patterns *(Step 1, opposite)*. When you draw them on the grid, you may want to create an original design by straightening out the curves to streamline the hall tree, or by accentuating curves to make it more whimsical. Be wary, though, of forming narrow segments or pointed tips that may break when you build or use the rack.

To shape the hooks and legs, you will need a saber saw designed for smooth cutting; choose a blade ¼ inch wide, with 8 to 10 teeth per inch. For making screw holes, use an electric drill with an adjustable counterbore bit for No. 10 Phillips screws. You can use a Phillips screwdriver to drive the screws into their holes, but a screwdriving attachment for a power drill will speed the job. You will need a C clamp to hold the pieces in place on a worktable during assembly. Be sure to have on hand small wood scraps to put between the clamp and the pieces of the rack, to prevent the jaws of the clamp from damaging the wood.

Once you have assembled the rack, you can finish it with low- or high-gloss paint — the rack at left has been painted with an alkyd primer-sealer and an alkyd flat-finish paint to give it a soft matte look — or you can apply an oil stain followed by satin varnish to highlight the grain of the wood.

Materials List

1 x 1	4 pieces baluster stock 1 x 1, each 54 " long
1 x 10	12 ' pine 1 x 10, grade D or better
Wood plugs	16 ⅜ " wood plugs, or 1 ⅜ " dowel sawed into 16 plugs, ¼ " long
Screws	16 No. 10 flat-head Phillips wood screws, 1¼ " long 16 No. 10 flat-head Phillips wood screws, 2 " long
Glue	yellow carpenter's glue
Finish	alkyd primer-sealer and alkyd flat-finish paint

This exploded view of the hall tree *(right)* shows how simply its parts fit together. When all four sections of the rack are assembled, an open, ¾-inch-square channel runs through the rack from top to bottom *(inset)*.

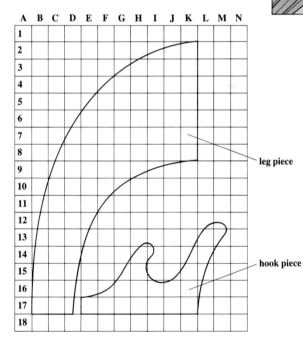

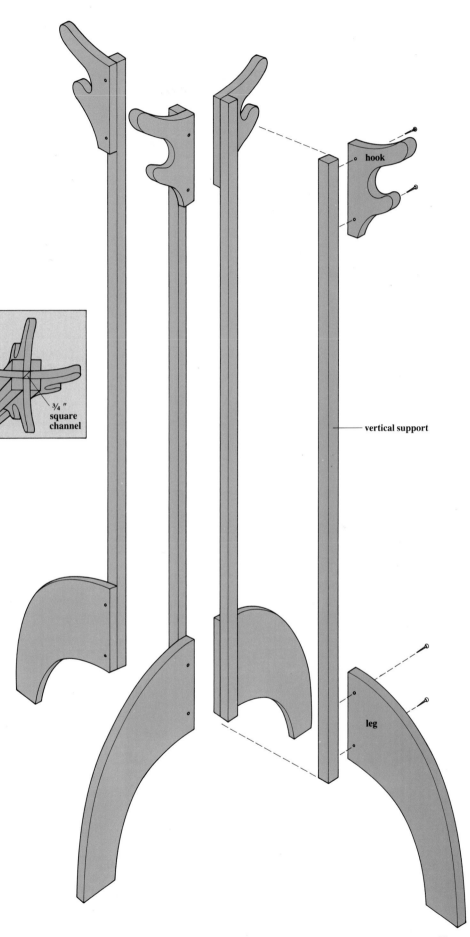

1 **Making leg and hook patterns.** Draw a grid of 1-inch squares on a 14-by-18-inch piece of lightweight cardboard. Letter the vertical lines and number the horizontals to match the grid shown above. Use the letters and numbers as coordinates to make tick marks on the cardboard at every point where the outlines of the leg and hook pieces cross the lines of this grid. Draw straight lines and smooth curves to connect the marks — using a flexible metal ruler stood on edge to guide your pencil along curves. Cut out the patterns with scissors.▶

49

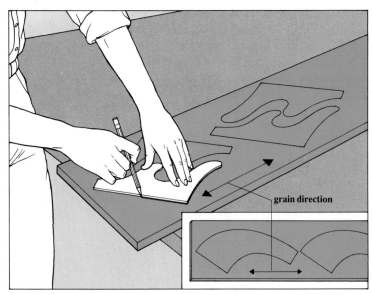

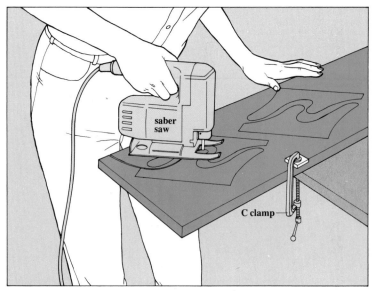

2 **Transferring the designs to wood.** Position the hook pattern on a 1-by-10 pine board so that the upward sweep of the hook runs in the same direction as the wood grain. Trace around the edge of the pattern with a pencil. Draw four hooks onto the board, positioning them carefully to avoid knots and to use as little wood as possible. Then draw four outlines of the leg piece on the board; align these pieces so the downward sweep of each leg runs in the same direction as the wood grain *(inset)*.

3 **Cutting out the pieces.** Position the marked board so that one outline hangs over the end of the worktable, and clamp the board in place with a C clamp. Fit a wood scrap between the clamp and the board to protect the wood's surface. Use a saber saw to cut out the overhanging piece, cutting from the edge of the board to the pencil line and then around the line. As you complete the cut, steady the piece with your hand to keep it from jumping. Cut out the other pieces, reclamping the board as necessary. Use coarse (60-grit) sandpaper to smooth the curves of the cut pieces. Then finish the curves and flat surfaces with medium (100-grit) sandpaper. Sand the 1-by-1 supports with medium sandpaper.

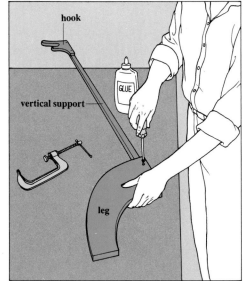

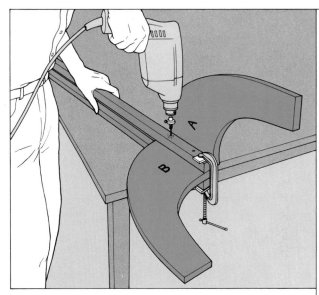

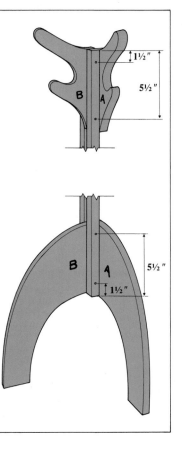

6 **Drilling and attaching legs and hooks.** Set the marked leg piece over the free end of the support to which the hook is attached. Align the bottom of the longer straight end of the leg with the bottom of the support, and clamp the two pieces together to the table. Drill holes at the marks, then glue and screw the leg to the support as you did the hook. Attach the remaining hooks and legs to vertical supports in the same way.

7 **Building the halves.** Lay one hook-and-leg assembly on the table with its vertical support underneath. Mark the hook and leg **B**. Mark another assembly **A**; position its support over that of the first. Clamp the pieces to the table. Mark the center of the upper support 1½ inches and 5½ inches from the top and bottom *(right)*. Adjust the drill bit so the shank hole will go through the support and the pilot hole will be 2 inches deep. Drill holes at the marks, unclamp the pieces, and glue and screw them together with 2-inch No. 10 flat-head Phillips screws. Join the other two assemblies similarly.

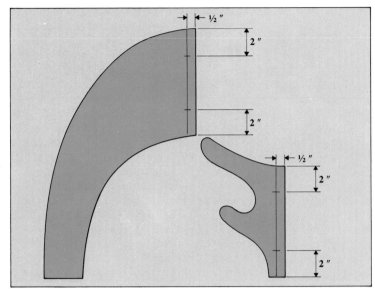

4 **Marking the pieces for screw holes.** Arrange one pair of hook and leg pieces at a time as shown above. Draw a light pencil line ½ inch from the right edge of each piece. Mark positions for screw holes 2 inches from the top and 2 inches from the bottom along each line.

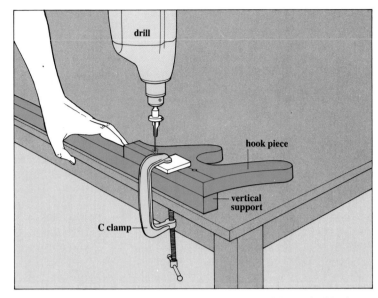

5 **Drilling and attaching a hook piece.** Align the top of the marked hook with the top of one support, and clamp the pieces to the table. Drill counterbored holes for No. 10 wood screws so that the screwheads will sit ¼ inch below the wood's surface *(page 122)*. Unclamp the pieces and apply wood glue to the part of the support that will contact the hook. Put the two pieces together again and drive a 1¼-inch No. 10 flat-head Phillips screw through each hole.

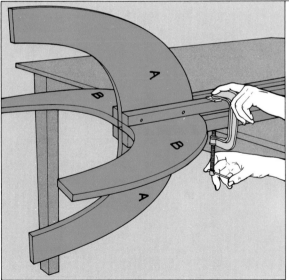

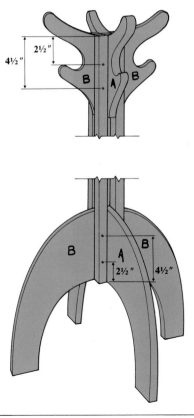

8 **Joining the halves.** Clamp the halves together with the vertical support of each **B** assembly abutting the hook and leg of an **A** assembly. Mark points along the center line of each vertical support of a **B** assembly 2½ inches and 4½ inches from the top and bottom *(right)*. Use the counterbore bit, set as it was for Step 7, to drill holes at these points through the supports into the hooks and legs. Unclamp the halves, apply glue and secure them with 2-inch screws.

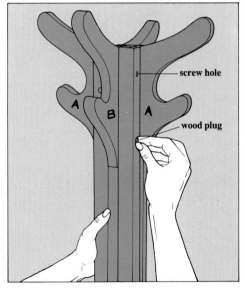

9 **Plugging the screw holes.** Squeeze glue onto a piece of cardboard. Dip one end of a wood plug into the glue, then press the plug into one screw hole. If the plug is too big, tap it lightly with a hammer. Wipe away excess glue with a damp cloth. Plug the remaining holes, and let the glue dry overnight. Sand the plugs flush with the surrounding wood. Wipe away all sanding dust, then apply paint or wood stain, following the manufacturer's instructions.

A versatile rack of fabric

Neat, handy storage for often-used tools and materials is the sober function of the gaily colored rack shown below. Assembling its lightweight parts — a wood frame and a foam-core board, wrapped by fabric that is fitted with straps of webbing and Velcro® tape (box, opposite) — requires only a staple gun and sewing machine. Since each rack is custom-designed for its contents (Step 4), the basic plan is adaptable to almost anything: sewing gear as here, workshop tools, hobby supplies, desk accessories, even vacuum-cleaner attachments.

The rack's frame consists of the interlocking wooden stretchers used for artists' canvases and available at any art-supply store. To keep the fabric from sagging, the frame is covered with a sheet of foam-core board — plastic foam that is sheathed in paper. The board should match the outside dimensions of the stretchers — here, 16 by 24 inches. It can be cut to size at the art-supply store, or at home with a sharp utility knife.

The best fabric for the rack is canvas. Most home sewing machines can handle medium-weight (11.5 ounces per square yard) canvas; consult your machine's manual before sewing heavier canvas, which may break ordinary sewing needles. If you cannot find suitable canvas, tightly woven drapery or upholstery fabric will suffice, provided it is reinforced with a matching piece of iron-on fusible interfacing. Whatever the fabric, choose a solid color or an intricate print; stripes, plaids and geometric patterns tend to distort as fabric is stretched.

The webbing for the straps is sold by the yard and in widths from ⅝ inch to 2 inches; the 1-inch webbing shown here will hold most articles. Polypropylene webbing, available from stores specializing in canvas or in outdoor furniture, is easiest to use because its ends can be heat-sealed. Cotton or polyester webbing, which is readily available from fabric stores, also is suitable, provided its cut ends are sewed to prevent unraveling.

The kind of strap used here provides great flexibility for hanging a group of items. It consists of a length of webbing with a Velcro hook tape all along it; this strap is laid across objects positioned on a matching Velcro loop tape that is sewn to the fabric. The remarkable holding strength of the Velcro fasteners — 5 pounds of pull per square inch of tape — is more than sufficient for household tools.

To augment the webbing straps, the frame itself can hold spools of thread and similar light objects on plain or decorative nails (below). Tap the nails through the fabric and foam-core board into the underlying stretcher. Spray the completed rack with an aerosol stain repellent. Mount it with one of the fasteners discussed on pages 124-125, securing both the top and bottom so that tugging on a strap will not pull the rack off the wall.

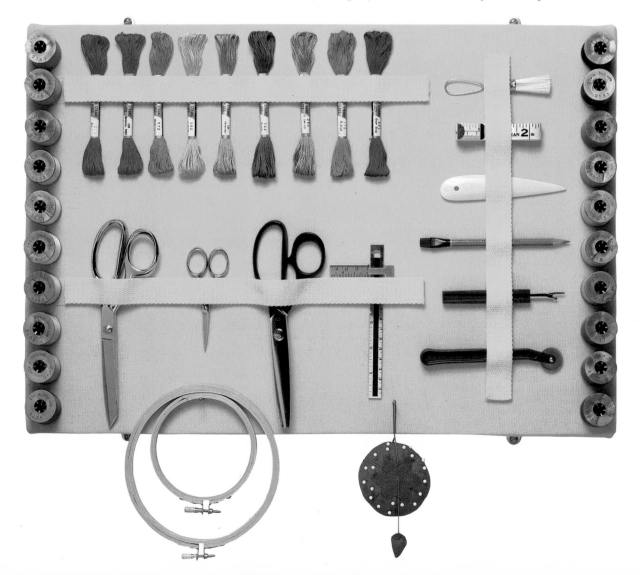

Materials List

Stretchers	2 stretcher bars, 16 ″ long 2 stretcher bars, 24 ″ long
Foam-core board	1 piece foam-core board, 16 ″ x 24 ″
Canvas	1 piece canvas, 22 ″ x 30 ″
Webbing	1½ yds. polypropylene webbing
Velcro	1½ yds. Velcro fastening tape
Nails	decorative brass nails, 1¼ ″ long

Ingenious Fastening Tape

The rack opposite uses versatile Velcro tapes, said to have been inspired by the common cocklebur, whose tiny hooks so readily snag sweaters and other loosely woven garments.

In Velcro fasteners, a rough hook tape *(top)* contains miniature rings of stiff monofilament nylon, all of them slit to create hooks. The complementary loop tape *(bottom)* is surfaced with soft, thickly piled nylon fibers. When the two tapes are pressed together, the hooks snag the loop fibers, locking the fastener. Peeling the tapes apart pulls the monofilament hooks straight and so lets the tapes separate.

Though Velcro fasteners come in many shapes, the most versatile form is a tape of various widths sold by the yard. Such tapes have a larger usable surface area than other shapes; they can be cut to length with scissors and securely sewn to webbing or directly to the rack's fabric *(Steps 5-6)*.

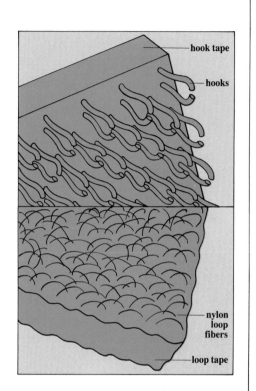

hook tape

hooks

nylon loop fibers

loop tape

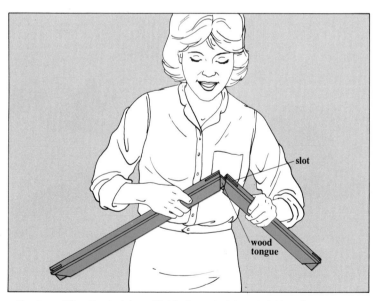

slot

wood tongue

1 **Assembling the stretchers.** Hold a long stretcher at right angles to a short one. Push the wood tongue at the end of each bar into the matching slot on the other bar until the mitered joint fits tightly together. Assemble the other pair of stretchers in the same way. Then fit together the ends of the resulting L-shaped assemblies to form a rectangular frame.

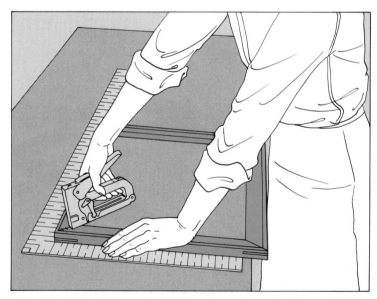

2 **Completing the frame.** Set the frame flat on the work surface and hold a carpenter's square against one corner at a time. If a corner is not perpendicular, push the stretchers against the square until the joint forms a perfect right angle. Hold the tip of a staple gun perpendicular to each corner joint, tilt the gun's heel up slightly and secure the joint with three ⁵⁄₁₆-inch staples spaced about ¼ inch apart.▶

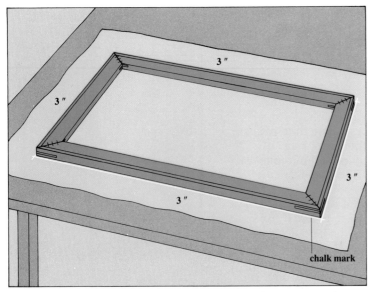

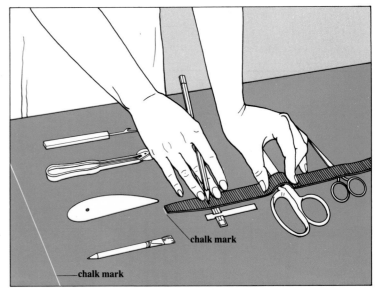

3 **Marking the fabric.** Lay a 22-by-30-inch piece of fabric on the work surface with its right side (the finished, more vividly colored one, if the two sides differ) upward. Center the frame on the fabric, leaving a 3-inch margin all around, and use dressmaker's chalk to draw a faint line onto the fabric along the sides of the frame.

4 **Laying out the rack.** Arrange the rack's future contents within the fabric's chalked outline. Run the webbing horizontally or vertically across the objects to be hung, pinching the webbing snugly around each item; leave at least 1½ inches extra at each end. Mark the fabric at each end of the planned strap, and cut the webbing to length. To seal polypropylene webbing, move the flame of a lighted match along each cut end for only two or three seconds, until the end barely begins to melt; finish the ends of cotton or polyester webbing with a zigzag stitch.

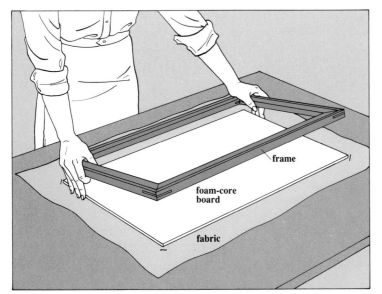

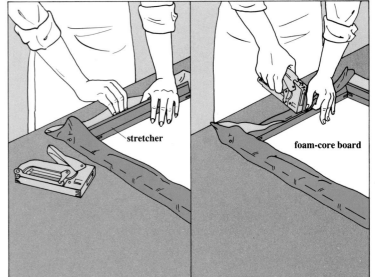

7 **Aligning the frame.** After sewing all of the loop tapes to the fabric (*Step 6*), mark each corner of the frame by pushing a pin through the fabric and back up again. Spread the fabric face-down on a tabletop. Put a 16-by-24-inch piece of foam-core board on the canvas, centering it within the pins. Then align the stretcher frame on the foam-core board.

8 **Stretching the fabric.** Fold, stretch and staple all four sides of the fabric. To do this, fold over 1 inch of fabric at the middle of the edge closest to you (*above, left*). Bring the fold over the frame, and staple it to the center of the stretcher (*above, right*). Rotate the frame 180° and fold the middle of the next edge, pulling the fabric taut. Staple it to the frame. Fold, stretch and staple the two other sides, then remove the four corner pins. Starting beside each center staple, fold the fabric and pull it taut over the stretcher; staple the fabric to the stretcher at 1½-inch intervals, stopping 2 inches from each corner.

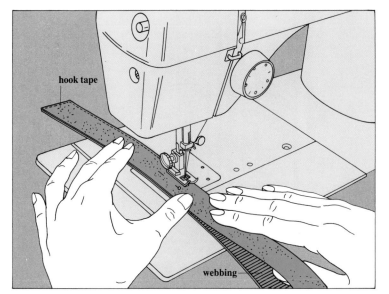

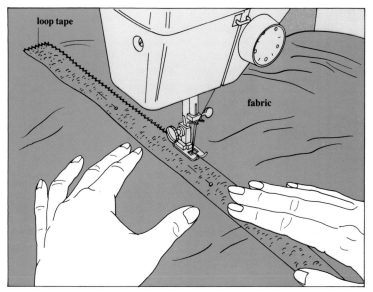
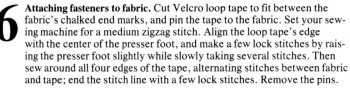

5 **Sewing fasteners to the webbing.** Cut a piece of Velcro hook tape to match the length of the webbing being sewn. Lay the webbing strip flat, and pin the hook tape to the strip. Set your sewing machine for a straight, regulation stitch (12 to 15 stitches per inch), then stitch along all four edges of the tape. For reinforcement at the beginning and end of the stitch line, backstitch by making three or four stitches in the reverse direction. Remove the pins.

6 **Attaching fasteners to fabric.** Cut Velcro loop tape to fit between the fabric's chalked end marks, and pin the tape to the fabric. Set your sewing machine for a medium zigzag stitch. Align the loop tape's edge with the center of the presser foot, and make a few lock stitches by raising the presser foot slightly while slowly taking several stitches. Then sew around all four edges of the tape, alternating stitches between fabric and tape; end the stitch line with a few lock stitches. Remove the pins.

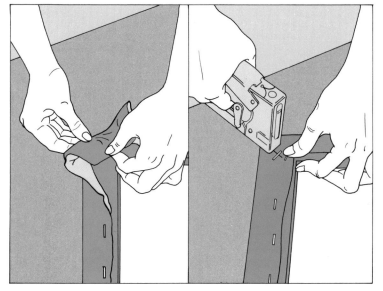

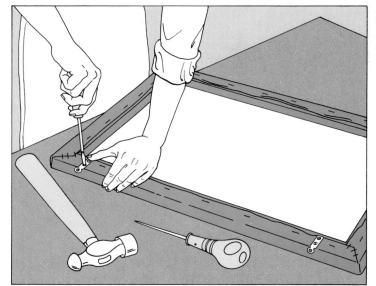
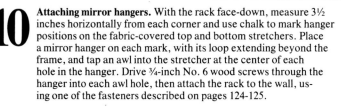

9 **Folding the corners.** Pull one corner of the fabric tightly over one of the frame's corners at a time. Fold the fabric corner under *(above, left)*, and staple the folded fabric to the frame. Neatly fold the fabric on one side of the corner into a flap, then fold the flap tightly over the frame and hold it down with one hand. Use the other hand to fold down another flap from the opposite side of the corner. Fasten the overlapping flaps with two staples *(above, right)*.

10 **Attaching mirror hangers.** With the rack face-down, measure 3½ inches horizontally from each corner and use chalk to mark hanger positions on the fabric-covered top and bottom stretchers. Place a mirror hanger on each mark, with its loop extending beyond the frame, and tap an awl into the stretcher at the center of each hole in the hanger. Drive ¾-inch No. 6 wood screws through the hanger into each awl hole, then attach the rack to the wall, using one of the fasteners described on pages 124-125.

A soft rack of pockets and loops

Bringing order to the chaos of a child's room begins with providing places for all the little things that would otherwise be clutter. One way to do it is with a colorful fabric rack like the one at right, which provides pockets and loops galore for toys and trinkets. Soft for safety, lightweight yet durable, it can be mounted on a wall or on the back of a door with wood dowels held by curtain-rod brackets.

The sewing techniques required are rudimentary; most stitching is done in straight lines. For the buttonholes, you need a machine that can do zigzag stitches, or a buttonhole attachment.

The fabric should be tight-woven and strong, as is the lightweight cotton shown here. Selecting a solid color or a tiny all-over pattern will simplify laying out the elements for cutting, and assembling them afterward. Fusible interfacing—a feltlike fabric with heat-activated adhesive on one side—can be pressed to the wrong side of the fabric, then sandwiched between folded layers to stiffen the body of the rack and the narrow buttonhole and loop strips. Two weights of interfacing are called for: heavy for the rack's body and lighter for the strips. Because interfacing is usually narrow, you will have to overlap it to cover the length of the rack.

Many fabrics cut fresh from the bolt are pulled out of shape by handling. To be sure woven threads meet at right angles and the pieces you cut are true rectangles, straighten the fabric before you cut it. Wash and press it, then make a small cut into the tight weave of the selvage edge near one end. From this cut, gently draw out a thread running perpendicular to the edge, letting the fabric pucker. Pull the thread out and smooth the fabric, then cut along the line left by the thread.

The fabric and the dimensions of this rack were chosen for the tiny items of a child's room. By using different fabric and measurements, you can design a rack to fit any room and hold any number of things. Always cut the back piece 2 inches wider than the finished size, to account for the 1-inch seam allowance—the fabric margin between a line of stitches and the cut edge—on each side.

This rack is hung from ¼-inch dowels that fit tightly into curtain-rod brackets. If you use dowels of another size, buy them ahead of time to be sure they will fit through the casings in the rack.

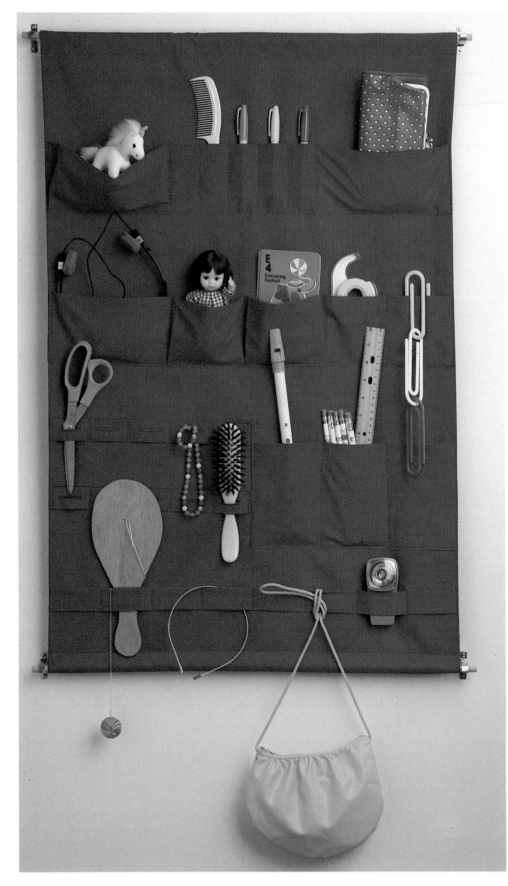

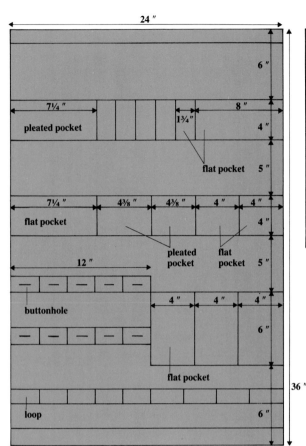

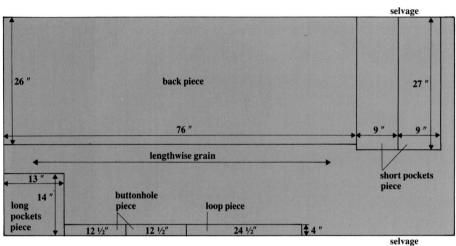

A fabric rack. When finished, the pocket rack *(left)* is 24 inches wide and 36 inches long. Each of the top two strips combines pleated and flat pockets. Below them are two strips of buttonholes and one of loops, plus a trio of long flat pockets. If the fabric is a solid color or has a tiny all-over pattern, all of the elements of the rack can be cut from 2¾ yards of 45-inch-wide fabric, as shown in the diagram above. Before cutting your fabric, use the measurements from the diagram to make a paper pattern; label each element, and cut it out on the lines. Then pin the pattern to the fabric; be sure to lay the buttonhole and loop elements along the selvage edge to minimize the need for lengthwise seams. If you change the dimensions of the rack, test-fold the patterns for pleated pockets to determine how much fabric to allow for pleats made by the technique demonstrated in Step 7, page 58.

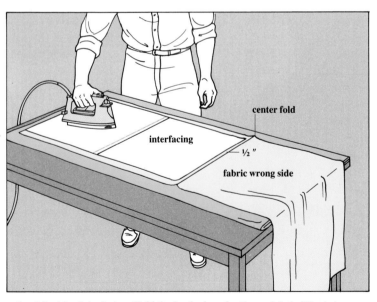

1 **Attaching interfacing.** Fold the back piece for the rack in half by bringing the two 26-inch ends together with the right-side faces touching. With a thick blanket or towel protecting the worktable, press the fold flat with a steam iron, then unfold the fabric right side down on the table. Position lengths of interfacing over one half of the back piece, leaving a ½-inch gap at the center fold. You will need more than one piece of interfacing to cover the back piece; overlap the lengthwise edges. Then use the iron to press the interfacing to the fabric *(above)*. Apply interfacing to the other half of the back piece in the same manner.

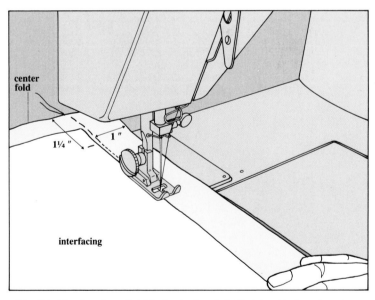

2 **Stitching the edges.** Fold the back piece in half, right-side faces together, along the pressed line. Use chalk to make a mark 1¼ inches from the center fold near both corners. Set your sewing machine for basting stitches — very long stitches that hold seams temporarily. Beginning at the fold, baste along one side of the piece, 1 inch from the cut edge; end the basting stitches at the chalk mark. Then set the machine for 12 stitches to the inch, and continue sewing 1 inch from the edge all the way down the side of the piece *(above)*. Repeat this procedure on the other side of the back piece. ▶

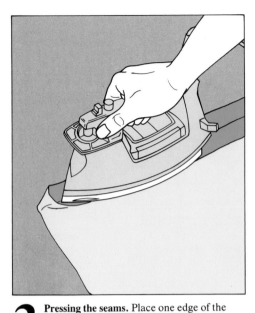

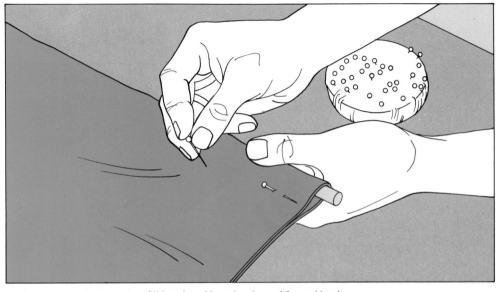

3 **Pressing the seams.** Place one edge of the back piece on an ironing board, fold back the top flap of the seam allowance and press it flat. Turn the piece over and press the other flap; do not worry about the small section at the center fold that will not lie flat. Repeat the pressing process on the seam at the opposite edge. Use a seam ripper to remove the basting stitches from the seams near the fold, then turn the back piece right side out and press it.

4 **Preparing the top casing.** Slide a dowel into the channel formed by the folded end of the back piece. Pin the two faces of the piece together with a line of pins parallel to the dowel; position the pins so that the dowel is held securely in the casing channel but can be moved easily in and out. Remove the dowel, and stitch along the pinned line; remove each pin just before the needle reaches it.

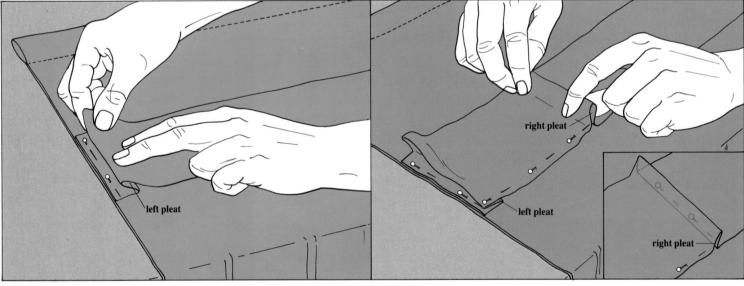

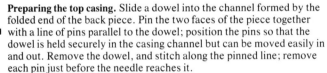

right pleat

left pleat

left pleat

right pleat

7 **Making a pleated pocket.** Pin the closed end of the pocket strip to the left-hand edge of the back piece, with the top edge of the strip 6 inches from the top of the back piece; be sure the seam of the strip faces the back piece. To make the left-hand pleat of the pocket, measure 1 inch from the pinned end and — using both hands — pinch a fold in the fabric strip. Then bring the strip back so the fold is flush with the pinned end *(above, left)*. Press this pleat in place with a steam iron. Pin the bottom of the strip to the back piece for 6 inches. To make the right-hand pleat, measure 7¼ inches from the pinned end and pinch another fold in the strip. Tuck the strip under the fold *(above)* and press in place. Secure the strip to the back piece with pins under the pleat *(inset)*.

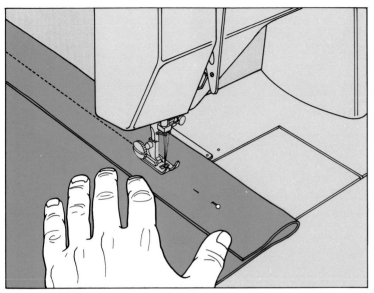

5 **Stitching the bottom casing.** Measure the top casing for the width of the opening. At the bottom of the back piece, fold the raw edge up toward the back and secure it with a line of pins parallel to the fold and at a distance corresponding to the width of the top casing opening. Insert a dowel in the channel this makes and, if necessary, adjust the pins for a good fit. Then stitch along the pinned line, removing pins as you go. Trim the raw edge of the folded hem with scissors.

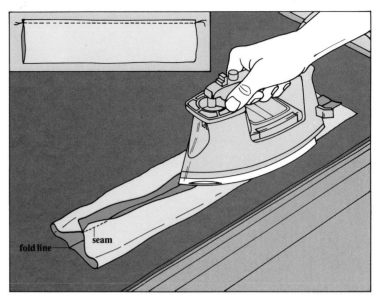

6 **Making pocket strips.** Fold one of the fabric pieces for a pocket strip in half lengthwise, with the right-side faces together, and press in the fold line. Sew the lengthwise edges together, leaving a seam allowance of ½ inch *(inset)*. Lay the strip on the ironing board, align the seam with the folded line, and spread the seam allowances flat with the steam iron. Stitch across one end of the strip, leaving a ½-inch seam allowance. Do not close the opposite end. Turn the panel right side out and press it.

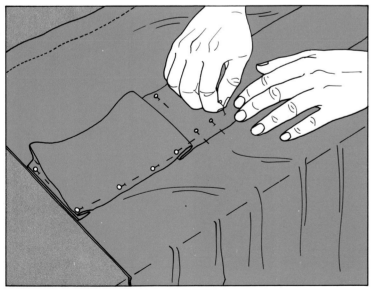

8 **Pinning flat pockets.** Secure the right-hand pleat with a pin through the pleat and back piece at the bottom edge of the fabric strip. Then measure along the bottom edge of the remaining section of the strip, and use pins to mark the positions of each of the flat pockets.

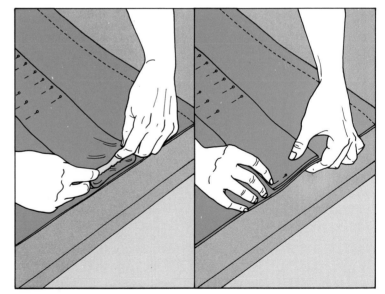

9 **Ending the pocket strip.** When you reach the right-hand side of the back piece, tuck the cut edge of the fabric strip into the open end *(above, left)*, and line up the tucked end with the rack's edge. Pin the end *(above, right)*. Position the remaining pocket strips on the back piece following the techniques demonstrated in Steps 7 through 9. Make sure to start each row of pockets by pinning the seamed end of the pocket strip to the back piece, and to complete the row with the tucked end. ▶

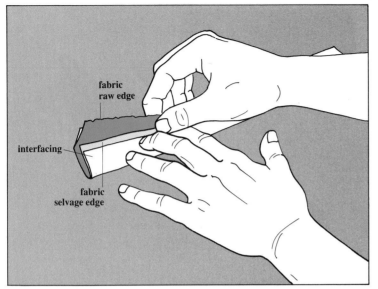

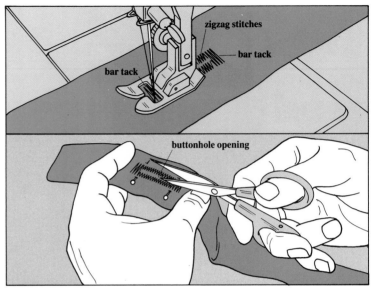

10 **Making a buttonhole strip.** Cut a piece of interfacing the same size as a buttonhole strip, then use the steam iron to press it onto the wrong side of the buttonhole strip. Turn the strip right side up and fold the selvage edge over so it is 2 inches from the raw edge. Then fold the raw edge over the selvage edge and use the iron to press the folds in place. Stitch across each end of the folded strip, ¼ inch from the edge. Then turn the strip right side out and press it flat with the iron. Draw lines on the buttonhole strip to indicate the length and position of each buttonhole. Make similar pieces for the other buttonhole strip and the loop strip.

11 **Making buttonholes.** Attach the zigzag foot and set the stitch length at 0 for bar-tack stitches. Position the needle at one end of a buttonhole and sew five or six bar tacks. Set the machine for a close zigzag stitch and sew along the left side of the marked line. Reset the machine and sew bar tacks. With the needle in the fabric, lift the presser foot and turn the fabric around, then lower the presser foot, and make zigzag stitches down the other side of the line *(top)*. After stitching the other buttonholes, pin the ends of each one at the bar-tack positions. Open each buttonhole by making short cuts with small scissors, from the center to the ends *(above, bottom)*. Make buttonholes in the other strip in the same manner.

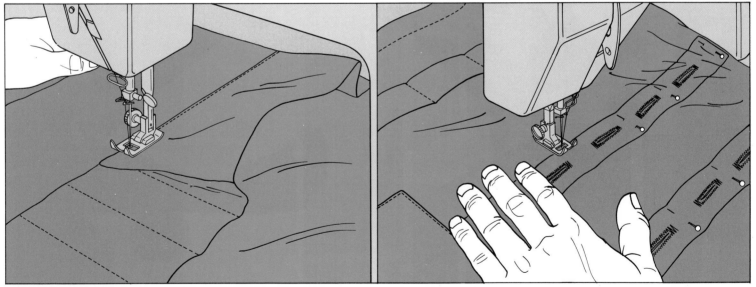

13 **Stitching down the pieces.** Reattach the standard presser foot to the machine and use regular stitches — 12 to the inch — to attach the strips to the back piece. Stitch one strip at a time along the pin lines, removing pins as you proceed. First stitch between the pockets of the top strip. Next, stitch along the bottom edge of the strip *(above, left)*. Stitch the second strip of pockets similarly. Then turn the rack around and sew lines of stitches along the lines marked with pins on the loop strip. Finally, stitch the remaining pockets and the buttonhole strips *(above, right)*.

12 Pinning buttonhole and loop strips. Attach the buttonhole strips to the back piece with pins at both ends and between each pair of buttonholes. Pin the loop strip at the ends and at 2½-inch intervals.

14 Mounting the rack. Slide dowels into the casings at the top and bottom of the rack. Using a carpenter's level and a straight-edge as guides, position two curtain-rod brackets 25 inches apart on a wall or the back of a door. Screw the brackets in place, then slip the ends of the top dowel into the brackets *(inset)*. Slip another bracket, upside down, over one end of the lower dowel; gently stretch the rack downward and mark the position of the bracket on the wall or door. Mount the bracket in this position, then position and mount the other bottom bracket in the same way. Slip the lower dowel under the bottom brackets.

A handy, handsome laundry bin

This laundry bin — with three boldly colored bags that make it easy even for small children to sort their own clothing — is actually two projects in one. The next five pages show you how to build the frame for the bags. Instructions for making the bags themselves begin on page 68.

Despite the seeming complexity of the multiangled frame, two tricks simplify its construction. One is to customize a miter box by sawing extra grooves (*Steps 1 and 2, opposite*); those grooves then enable you to cut all the boards precisely to the angle required. The other special technique is the use of a template to position

holes for the dowels that span the frame. A full-sized pattern for the template appears on page 65, Step 7. You need only trace it, cut out your template and use it to mark drilling locations.

With the miter box and template — and diligent attention to detail — you can create a frame as neatly put together as the one shown here. Be precise when marking and drilling the dowel holes. The holes are very close to one another and to the edges of the boards; a misdirected drill bit could break through the side of a hole. A drill guide fitted to your power drill will minimize the possibility of error.

The boards are clear pine 1-by-3s, sold

in 8-foot lengths. Before sawing the angled ends, cut the boards to manageable sizes (*Materials List, opposite*). You can get all the pieces from five 8-foot lengths: Cut a 51-inch and a 38-inch board from each of two 8-footers; then cut three 30-inch boards from each of two more 8-footers; finally, cut the last two 30-inch segments from the fifth 8-footer.

The 1-inch-diameter dowels are glued into their holes to hold the two side sections of the frame together. To make sure they will fit snugly, drill a 1-inch hole in scrap wood, take it to the lumberyard and test the dowels. If they fit too loosely, buy slightly larger dowels and sand their ends.

Materials List (for the frame)

1 x 3	5 clear pine 1 x 3s, 8 ' long, cut into:
	8 pieces, 30 " long 2 pieces, 51 " long 2 pieces, 38 " long
Dowels	3 1 " dowels, 4 ' long, cut into:
	4 rods, 22¾ " long 2 rods, 21¼ " long
	3 ⅝ " dowels, 4 ' long, cut into:
	4 rods, 23¼ " long 2 rods, 21¾ " long
Casters	4 spherical steel casters with 2 " wheels, plastic treads, flat steel plates and a rated load capacity of 75 lbs. per caster, with 16 No. 6 wood screws, ¾ " long

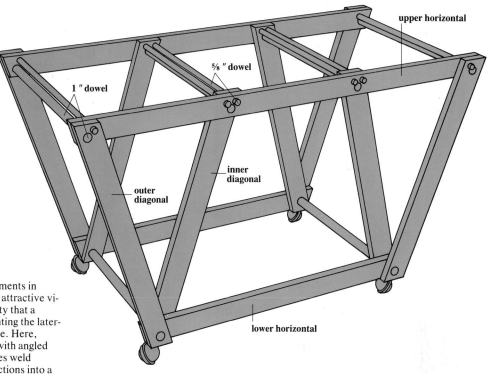

A sturdy frame of rods and angled boards. The triangular elements in the design of this laundry-bin framework provide more than attractive visual rhythm; they also give the frame the same kind of rigidity that a truss bridge derives from similar structural triangles, preventing the lateral movement that could cause a rectangular frame to collapse. Here, the diagonals and horizontals are made from 1-by-3 boards with angled ends. Six 1-inch-diameter dowels glued into snug-fitting holes weld the boards of each side section together and bind the two sections into a single unit. The laundry bags hang from other dowels, ⅝ inch in diameter, which fit loosely in their holes so they can be slipped in and out. Casters that swivel in any direction make the whole bin easy to move about, even when heavily loaded with laundry ready for the wash.

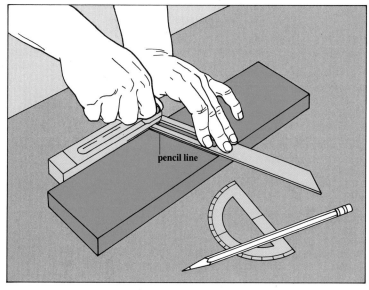

1 Setting a T bevel at the cutting angle. To cut the 1-by-3s at the required 107° angle, first use a pencil to mark a point on the straight edge of a piece of scrap wood. Lay a protractor on the wood, aligning its base with the edge and positioning its center point against the pencil mark. On the protractor scale that reads from right to left, find 107° and mark that point on the wood. Connect that point to the edge mark with a straight line. Now hold the handle of a T bevel against the edge of the wood while you align the long edge of its blade with the 107° line *(above)*. Tighten the nut on the T bevel's handle to hold the blade in that position.

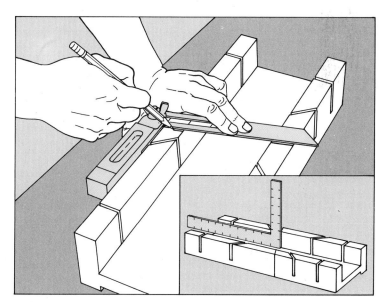

2 Preparing the miter box. With the handle of the T bevel hard against the side of the miter box, draw a pencil mark across each of the two top edges of the box where the T bevel's blade rests *(above)*. Using a steel square, draw perpendicular lines from the near ends of the pencil marks down the sides of the miter box *(inset)*. Use a backsaw to cut a groove in the box, following the pencil lines. Keep the saw blade cutting straight down the perpendicular lines, so you do not saw a slanted groove. ▶

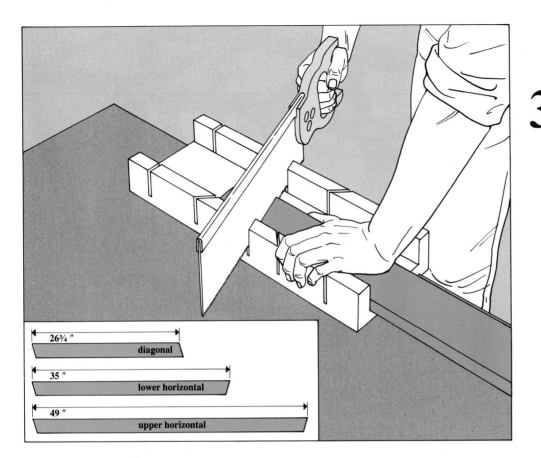

26¾ "	
diagonal	
35 "	
lower horizontal	
49 "	
upper horizontal	

3 Cutting boards for the frame. To make each diagonal, first lay a 30-inch-long 1-by-3 flat in the miter box, and slide it along until its right-hand end extends about an inch beyond the groove you cut in the near side of the box. Push the board hard against the back wall of the box, and cut off the end with a backsaw inserted in the newly made grooves *(left)*. Measure 26¾ inches along the edge of the board from the acute angle of the newly cut end, and mark that point with a pencil.

Now turn the board around — keeping the same face of the wood up — so that the end you just cut is to your left. Push the board against the back wall of the box, align the pencil mark with the left-hand edge of the sawing groove in that wall and make the second cut — parallel to the first *(inset)*. Saw the seven other diagonals the same way. Then saw the horizontals according to the measurements in the inset, turning each board over between cuts in order to produce the opposing angles shown.

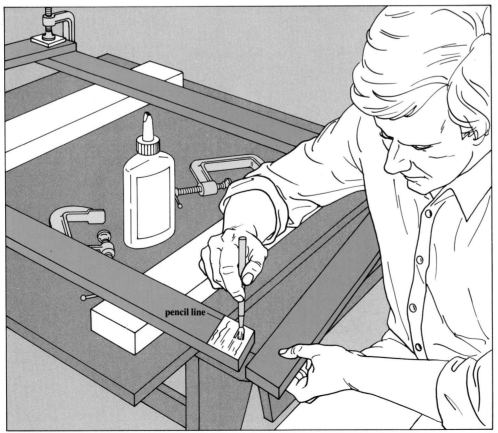

pencil line

5 Gluing the outer diagonals. Tighten the clamps at one end of the horizontals. Remove the clamps at the other end and lift off the diagonal. Spread a small amount of wood glue evenly on the exposed corner surfaces of the horizontals, between the ends of the boards and the pencil marks you made in Step 4. Using the marks as a guide, replace the diagonal; clamp it lightly. Then unclamp, glue and reclamp the diagonal at the other end of the horizontals. Work quickly so the boards can be adjusted before the glue takes hold; check the cater-cornered measurements again to make sure they are equal. Now tighten all the clamps and wait an hour for the glue to dry.

4 **Assembling the first boards.** To provide clearance for the clamps that will hold the boards together, place two long 2-by-4s on a large, flat work surface. Then position the upper and lower horizontals parallel to each other on the 2-by-4s so the distance from the outer edge of one to the outer edge of the other is 25½ inches. Place one diagonal across the left ends of the parallel horizontals. Match its outside corners and edges to theirs as closely as possible. Place another diagonal across the opposite ends, again matching outside corners and edges. Using scrap wood to protect the boards, clamp all the corners lightly.

Check the positions by measuring cater-cornered between two inside corners as shown, then measuring cater-cornered between the other two inside corners. The two distances should be identical. If they are not, shift the diagonals to compensate. Mark the placement of the diagonals on the horizontals with a pencil.

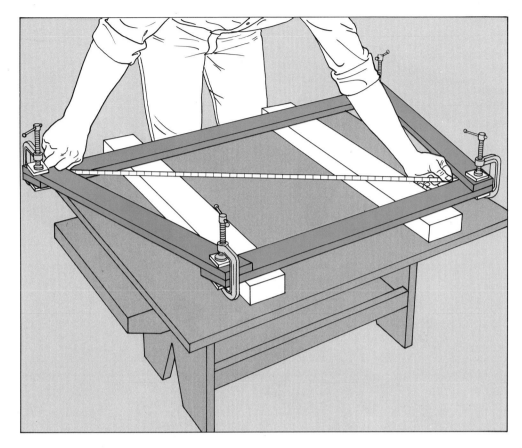

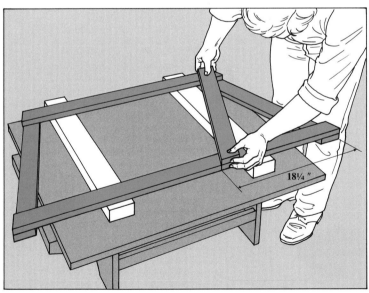

6 **Positioning the inner diagonals.** Remove the clamps. Turn the glued assembly over so the outer diagonals lie underneath the horizontals. Measure 18¼ inches along the outer edge of the upper horizontal from one acute corner, and mark that point. Position a diagonal (*above*) with one acute angle on the mark and the other acute angle on the outer corner of the lower horizontal, so that the ends of the diagonal are flush with the outer side edges of the horizontals. Position the other inner diagonal similarly. Glue and clamp the diagonals. After the glue has dried for an hour, remove the clamps and use them to assemble the other section of the frame, starting with Step 4. Then wait 24 hours for the glue to cure.

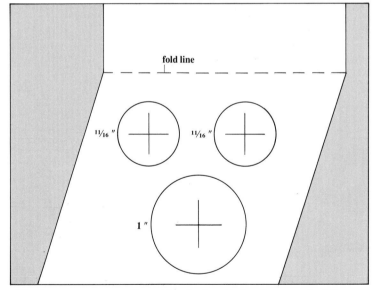

7 **Making a template.** To position the dowel holes, first trace the full-sized pattern above. The large circles represent holes you will drill with a 1-inch spade bit, and the smaller circles represent holes you will drill with an $^{11}/_{16}$-inch bit. The cross at the center of each circle marks the point where the tip of the bit is to be positioned when drilling starts. Cut the template out along the solid outside lines. Fold and crease it along the dotted line; the fold will enable you to fit the paper pattern securely over a section of the frame. ▶

8 **Marking the upper dowel holes.** Put one section of the frame on the work surface, with the inner diagonals on top. Place the template over the upper end of an inner diagonal as shown, aligning the template's edges with the edges of the 1-by-3 and turning the fold over the end of the board. With an awl, pierce the paper and dent the wood at each circle's center cross; mark on the board which dents are for the $1\frac{1}{16}$-inch bit and which for the 1-inch bit.

Now move the template to the far end of the upper horizontal, matching the pattern's acute angle and edges to those of the horizontal's corner. Here, mark the large hole and only the inside small hole, the one farthest from the end of the horizontal. Then turn the template face down, and use it to mark the other inner diagonal and the other end of the upper horizontal in the same way, so they appear as a mirror image of the first two.

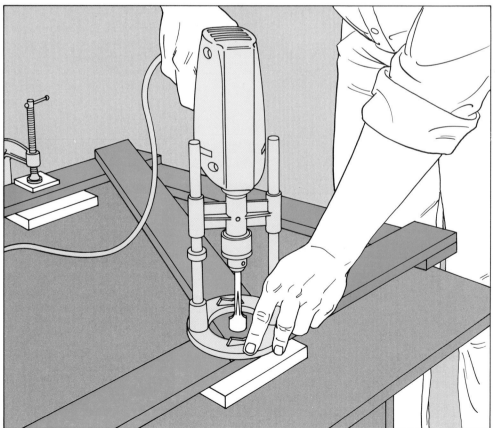

10 **Drilling the dowel holes.** Lay one side of the frame, inner diagonals facing up, on the worktable. Put scraps of lumber ¾ inch thick (actual, not nominal, thickness) on the table beneath the upper horizontal where it joins the inner diagonals. Place two other ¾-inch scraps beneath the lower horizontal. Clamp the lower horizontal and its scraps to the table, protecting the frame's upper face with small wood scraps. Using a drill guide and a 1-inch spade bit, drill straight down through each inner diagonal and the upper horizontal at the dent for the 1-inch hole. Use an $1\frac{1}{16}$-inch bit to bore the two smaller holes through each joint in the same way.

Unclamp the frame. Place ¾-inch-thick scraps beneath the ends and the center of each outer diagonal, and clamp the diagonal's center to the table. At each corner, drill the marked holes through the frame's pieces. Remove this side of the frame, and drill the other side in the same way. Lightly sand the interior of each hole.

9 **Marking the other dowel holes.** Draw a straight line across the lower face of an inner diagonal, parallel to the bottom edge of the board and 1 inch from the edge. Along that line, measure 1 inch from the outer side edge of the diagonal (*right*) and make a dent there with an awl; that is where you will place the tip of the 1-inch bit to drill a dowel hole. Mark the base of the other inner diagonal in the same way. Now remove this section of the frame, place the other one on the table and mark dowel-hole positions on it to match.

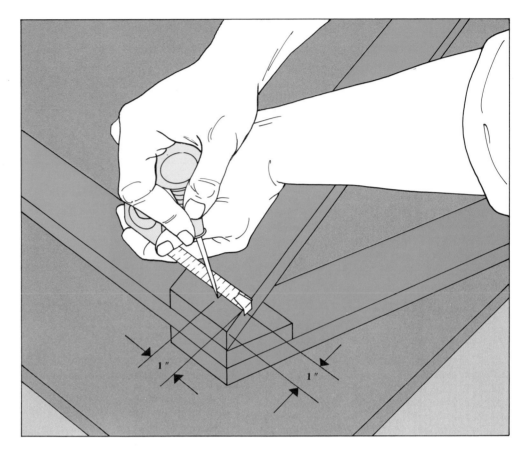

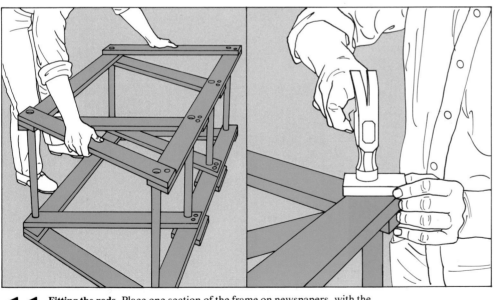

11 **Fitting the rods.** Place one section of the frame on newspapers, with the inner diagonals facing up. Brush glue into the six 1-inch dowel holes. Push the four long dowels into the holes at the four corners, and the two short ones into the holes near the center of the upper horizontal; place ¾-inch-thick scrap wood under the last two holes to support the horizontal there. Now brush glue into the 1-inch dowel holes of the other section of the frame. Holding that section with the outer diagonals facing up, set it onto the standing dowels (*above, left*). By hand, fit each rod into its hole. Then use a hammer and a block of wood to tap the frame at each dowel position (*above, right*) until the tips of the rods are flush with the surface of the boards. Allow the glue to dry for at least 24 hours.

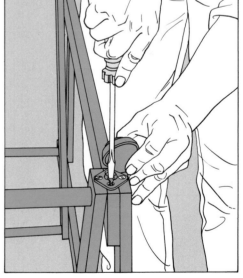

12 **Attaching the casters.** Sand the edges and sharp corners of the frame. Then sand the four corner bases with 80-grit sandpaper until they are smooth. Position the plate of a ball caster over the edges of a base as shown above, and mark the four screw holes with a pencil. Drill pilot holes (*page 122*) to fit ¾-inch No. 6 wood screws, and use screws that size to mount the caster to the base. Attach the other three casters in the same way.

Simple Steps to a Sturdy Bag

The laundry bags shown on page 62 are made of a blended cotton-and-polyester fabric; but any sturdy, tightly woven, washable fabric of medium to heavy weight could be substituted. If you use a natural fabric, such as cotton, be sure to straighten the grain if necessary *(page 56)*. Even if you do not need to straighten the grain, wash and press the fabric to guard against shrinkage and to remove the resin sizing applied by manufacturers.

The instructions that follow are for one bag. When completed, it will measure 22 inches from opening to bottom, 18 inches across each side, and 14 inches across the front and back. Use the diagram on the opposite page to mark and cut the fabric.

When pin-basting two pieces together, insert the pins with their heads toward the edge of the material, and take only a small bite through the fabric, so that all but a tiny midsection of each pin is on top. Never try to sew over pins. Always pull them out just before the sewing machine needle reaches them; pins can dull needles or break them, throwing off dangerous fragments.

Except when otherwise noted in the instructions, keep your machine set for a regulation stitch (12 to 15 stitches per inch) appropriate to the fabric you are using. Always begin and end a line of stitches by backstitching *(page 123)*.

When you finish the bags, iron out all the wrinkles. If you want the bags to hang neatly whether they are empty or full, you may cut a sheet of ¼-inch-thick acrylic or hardboard to size, and place it in the bottom of each one.

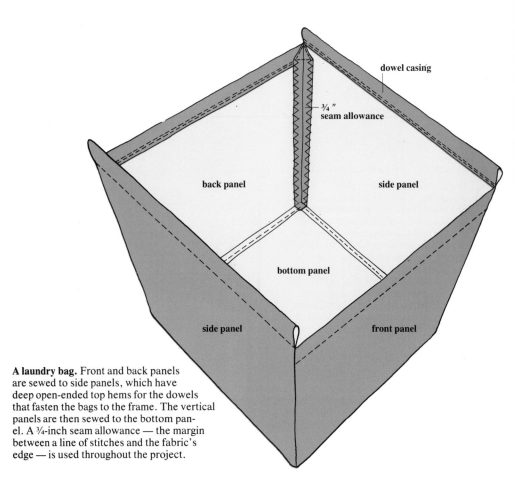

A laundry bag. Front and back panels are sewed to side panels, which have deep open-ended top hems for the dowels that fasten the bags to the frame. The vertical panels are then sewed to the bottom panel. A ¾-inch seam allowance — the margin between a line of stitches and the fabric's edge — is used throughout the project.

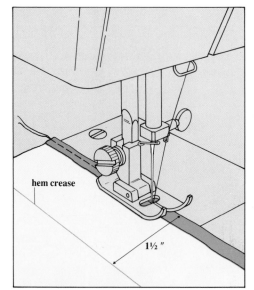

1 **Finishing the top hem edges.** With the front panel's right — usually brighter — side face down on an ironing surface, measure and fold a 1¾-inch margin at the top. Press with a steam iron; the crease will be the hemline. Fold and press the back and side panels similarly. Unfold one panel at a time face down on a sewing machine, and stitch ¼ inch from the top's raw edge. Fold along the stitch line and sew another line *(above)*, ⅛ inch from that fold.

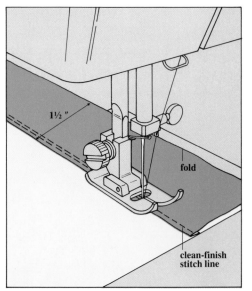

2 **Stitching a hem in place.** Fold the hem of the front panel down again toward the wrong — or duller — side of the fabric along its creased line. Sew the hem in place with a row of stitches parallel to and close to the finished edge. Then fold and stitch down the hem of the back panel.

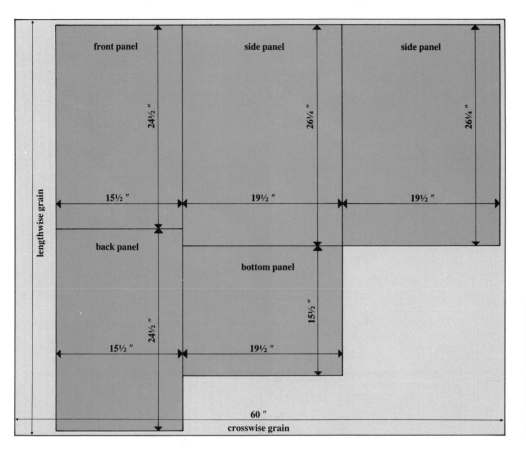

front panel

side panel

side panel

24½"

26¼"

26¼"

lengthwise grain

15½"

19½"

19½"

back panel

bottom panel

24½"

15½"

15½"

19½"

60"

crosswise grain

A layout for cutting fabric. Using the pattern provided here as a guide, you can cut all the panels for one bag from less than 1½ yards of 60-inch-wide fabric. Mark a large sheet of paper with the exact measurements and lines that appear in the diagram. Label each panel on the paper, and cut out the pieces. Then pin the patterns to the fabric, making sure that the longitudinal lines of the vertical pieces follow the lengthwise grain of the fabric. Cut the fabric, following the outline of the paper patterns.

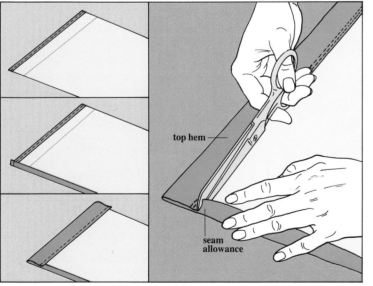

top hem

seam allowance

3 **Clipping the seam allowance.** To make the dowel casing at the top of a side panel, first lay the panel right side down and unfold the pressed top hem *(top inset)*. Then, along each long side edge, fold and press with a steam iron a ¾-inch-wide seam allowance extending 5 inches down from the top edge *(middle inset)*. Fold the top hem down again along its creased line *(bottom inset)*. With scissors, clip across the seam allowance along the bottom of the finished edge of the folded hem *(above)*. This small cut frees the seam allowance so that the front and back panels can be sewed to the side panels after the dowel casing is completed.

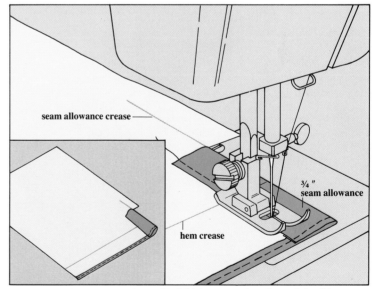

seam allowance crease

¾" seam allowance

hem crease

4 **Finishing the dowel casing.** Unfold the pressed top hem of the side panel *(inset)*. Starting the stitches where the seam allowance was clipped, sew the seam allowance at the top of the panel in place *(above)*; stitch close to the raw edge of the seam allowance so that the edge does not ravel when dowels are inserted and withdrawn. Sew the clipped seam allowance at the top of the other long edge of the panel in the same way. Then turn the top hem down at the crease, and stitch it in place as shown in Step 2, sewing across the stitch lines of the seam allowances. Finish the dowel casing of the other side panel in the same manner. ▶

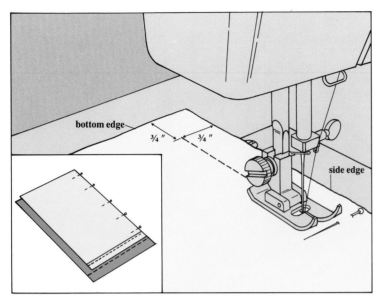

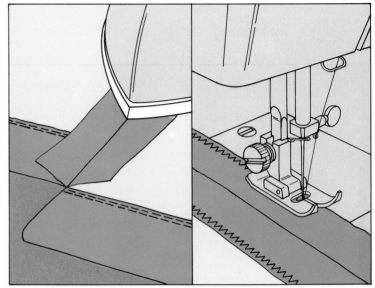

5 **Sewing panels together.** With the fabric's right sides face to face, align and pin one long edge of the front panel to a long edge of a side panel (*inset*). Attach the back panel and the other side panel with pins to make an open-ended, inside-out version of the finished bag. Starting ¾ inch from the bottom edge, stitch two panels together ¾ inch from the paired side edges (*above*) until you reach the top of the shorter panel. Stitch the other three paired edges similarly.

6 **Finishing the seams.** Press each side seam open with an iron (*above, left*). Then position one edge of a seam allowance under the sewing machine's needle. Make sure that you are working with a single thickness of fabric; keep the rest of the material away from the path of the needle. Set your machine for a zigzag stitch, and sew the whole length of the raw edge (*above, right*). Finish all the seam edges in the same way.

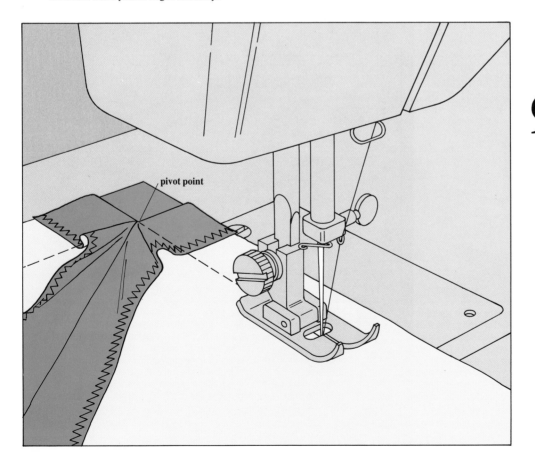

9 **Pivoting at a corner.** Place one pinned seam under the needle, keeping the bottom panel against the machine's bed. Set the machine for short stitches (16 to 20 stitches per inch); they provide a stronger seam. Starting from the center point of the seam allowance, sew a row of stitches ¾ inches from the raw edge. Remove pins before the needle reaches them. As you approach the corner, stitch across the bottom flap of the vertical panel's seam allowance.

Then stop at the point where the vertical seam allowances split to reveal a small corner square of the right side of the bottom panel. Do not sew into this square. Instead, leaving the needle in the fabric, raise the presser foot and turn the fabric a full 90° to the bag's adjacent side. Then flip the presser foot down again, stitch across that vertical seam allowance and continue sewing the bottom seam ¾ inch from the raw edge (*left*). Repeat the pivoting step each time you reach a corner.

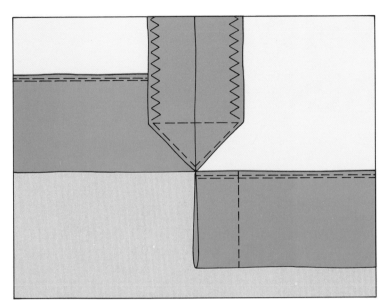

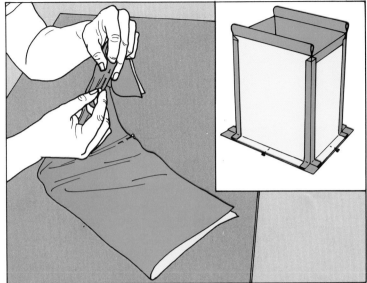

7 **Mitering the seam edge.** At the top of each seam allowance, fold the two free corner flaps under diagonally, aligning their top edges with the seam. Using a regulation straight stitch, sew the folded flaps to the panels in a triangular pattern *(above);* a triangle of stitches will show on the bag's outer surface. Finish the top corners of all four seams this way.

8 **Attaching bottom panel.** Fold the bottom panel crosswise in half and insert pins perpendicular to the fabric's edge at the center points of both ends of the fold. Unfold and spread flat. Fold the panel lengthwise in half, and pin those center points *(above).* Next, fold each vertical panel lengthwise in half, and pin the center. Then — making sure that the right sides of the fabric are facing each other and that the long edges of the bottom panel are matched to the side panels — align the pins of the bottom with those of the vertical panels shown in the inset. Now add more pins to hold the bottom panel in position.

10 **Finishing the job.** Turn the bag right side out, and press the bottom seam allowances flat onto the bottom panel. Work the bottom panel, wrong side up, under the presser foot. Making sure the needle is penetrating the two pressed-down seam allowances as well as the bottom itself, stitch along the four edges of the bottom panel, about ¼ inch in from the seam *(right).* To hang the bag, slide a ⅝-inch dowel through one of the open holes from the outside of the frame. Feed the rod through the side panel's tubelike top hem and into the hole on the other side of the frame. Insert a dowel rod into the other side panel's hem in the same way.

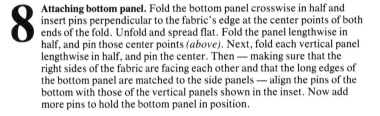

stitch line

A diversity of boxes

Boxes are indispensable as repositories for everything from wet boots and clean rags to valuable records and priceless mementos. The most common are probably simple rectangular wood or cardboard containers with a hinged or removable top. As the following pages show, however, variations on the box theme can produce elegant furniture with hidden storage space, or customized containers for special equipment, or convenient bins tailored to unusual spaces.

The materials that make up a box may vary as much as the design; almost anything you can shape into a hollow receptacle will do. Wood of one kind or another is particularly adaptable and generally is the material of choice for long-lived boxes, although acrylic plastic affords a wet-look slickness and poster-bright colors (pages 112-117). In choosing wood, you will have to consider such factors as strength, size, appearance of the finished product and the cost of the material (chart, opposite).

For example, if you want the rich, warm tones of natural wood and expense is no object, you can pick hardwood finish lumber; less expensive softwood finish lumber usually exhibits a less attractive grain pattern. Hardwood plywood is also more economical than hardwood lumber; it produces a similar appearance and lets you make a wide surface from a single sheet rather than several boards.

If the finished box is to be painted, you can choose from a greater selection of materials. Lightweight hardboard provides a smooth surface, but it is not strong enough to sit on or to support heavy objects; much heavier particleboard is stronger, but with a rough surface. Construction plywood is lighter than particleboard and also strong; its surface quality depends on the type and grade you select.

Wood sizes vary as the materials do. Finish lumber is solid, natural wood cut into boards. Boards are sold in nominal sizes of 1 to 2 inches thick by 1 to 12 inches wide — measurements that represent their size when first cut. The manufacturing process that produces a smooth board makes its actual measurements less; for example, a nominal 1-by-4 measures ¾ inch by 3½ inches. Three types of manufactured panels are also suggested for the projects on the following pages — plywood, particleboard and hardboard. All are most commonly sold as sheets 4 feet by 8 feet, in a variety of thicknesses; in some cases, lumberyards carry 4-by-4-foot sheets.

Finish lumber is generally more expensive than manufactured panels, and the best grades of any wood product are also the most expensive. Although a specific material is suggested for each project, you can substitute another type or use a less expensive grade; the differences are largely cosmetic, not structural.

The finish lumber called for in these projects is top-quality softwood, rated clear, or select, by lumber dealers. Within this rating, boards are graded A, B, C or D. Grades A and B yield a beautiful surface if stained, oiled or varnished. Grades C and D have smooth but imperfect surfaces; they are better suited for finishing with paint.

Plywood is a strong panel made of thin sheets of wood glued together. Hardwood plywood has hardwood veneers on both sides, birch being most common. Its faces are rated according to quality: An A face has a smooth, attractive pattern suitable for natural finish; a B face may have less-uniform color, with occasional streaks. A face graded 2, or sound, may have visible defects, but it is smooth and suitable for painting. A panel rated AA can be given a natural finish on both faces; less expensive, but just as good where only one face is visible, is a panel rated A2.

Construction plywood is generally less expensive than hardwood plywood. Its softwood surface veneers usually have a distinct, wavy grain that is accentuated by oiling or staining; the texture of the grain may even show through paint. The faces of construction plywood are graded A, B, C and D; panels rated AA or AB are suitable for storage boxes; use an AC panel only when the C face will be hidden, as in the upholstered banquette (pages 100-111).

Particleboard is made of wood chips mixed with adhesive and pressed into panels. It is inexpensive, easy to cut and has a uniform, speckled surface that is free of defects. Particleboard should be used only where surface appearance is unimportant, or if it will be painted. Since particleboard is about twice as heavy as plywood of the same thickness, it should not be used for building pieces that will be moved frequently.

To prepare a surface for a finish, fill the screw holes and any dents, knots and cracks at joints. If you are going to paint the surface, you can fill with spackle; if you plan a natural finish, use dowel plugs *(page 51)* for the screw holes, and wood putty that matches the surface to correct other imperfections.

Some surfaces present special problems. To avoid a pebbly finish, particleboard must be coated before painting with a thin layer of spackle, the excess scraped off with a flexible putty knife. To smooth the cut grain at the edges of particleboard or plywood before painting, work spackle in with a putty knife. For a more attractive edge on plywood that is to receive a natural finish, nail parting bead *(page 33)* to the edge and fill the nail holes with wood putty.

Before applying any kind of finish, sand the surface smooth, dust it with a damp rag, and apply the sealer recommended by the finish manufacturer. You will need to use shellac to seal particleboard, in order to prevent solvents in the paint from dissolving adhesives in the board. You should also use shellac to cover knots and pitch spots in construction plywood, to prevent their color from bleeding through the paint.

A Guide to Wood Types

SOFTWOOD LUMBER	*DIMENSIONS*	Nominal thickness 1 to 3 inches; nominal width 2 to 12 inches; board length 8 to 20 feet in 2-foot increments.
	SURFACE	Smooth and clear; light-colored; pronounced grain pattern; porous texture; grades C and D may have knots but no holes or cracks.
	SUITABLE FINISHES	Stain, oil, varnish or paint.
	COMMENTS	Usually white pine or spruce. Edges may be sanded; cut ends may be banded for smooth finish.
HARDWOOD LUMBER	*DIMENSIONS*	Nominal thickness ⅜ to 4 inches; lengths and widths random. Minimum lengths and widths vary with grade.
	SURFACE	Smooth and clear; beautiful grain patterns; various colors; extremely dense to porous texture; select and common grades may have one poorer side.
	SUITABLE FINISHES	Stain, oil or varnish.
	COMMENTS	Many wood species available; choose type for desired appearance. Select individual pieces for specific needs of project.
CONSTRUCTION PLYWOOD	*DIMENSIONS*	Thickness ¼ to 1¼ inches; panel width 3, 4 or 5 feet; length 5 to 12 feet; standard is 4 by 8 feet.
	SURFACE	Ranges from smooth surface to one with cracks and holes, depending on grade; light-colored; porous texture; may have one poorer side.
	SUITABLE FINISHES	Stain, varnish or paint.
	COMMENTS	Pronounced, wavy surface grain may show through paint. Edges should be filled, or banded if finish is natural.
HARDWOOD PLYWOOD	*DIMENSIONS*	Thickness ⅛ to ¾ inch; panel width 3 to 6 feet; length 4 to 12 feet; standard panel is 4 by 8 feet.
	SURFACE	Smooth and clear in most grades; varied colors and texture; sound grade may have streaks or knots but no holes; may have one poorer side.
	SUITABLE FINISHES	Stain, oil, varnish or paint.
	COMMENTS	Many species available; birch is most common. Edges should be banded, or filled if finish is paint.
PARTICLEBOARD	*DIMENSIONS*	Thickness ¼ to 2 inches; panel width 2 to 5 feet; length 4 to 16 feet; standard panel is 4 by 8 feet.
	SURFACE	Uniform, slightly pebbled, speckled appearance; yellowish in color.
	SUITABLE FINISH	Paint.
	COMMENTS	Eastern, high-density board is strongest. Heavy weight. Easy to cut and drill. Surface and edges should be filled and sealed with shellac before finishing.
HARDBOARD	*DIMENSIONS*	Thickness 1/16 to ¾ inch; panel width 4 to 5 feet; length 6 to 12 feet; standard panel is 4 by 8 feet.
	SURFACE	Uniform; one or both sides may be very smooth; generally dark brown in color.
	SUITABLE FINISH	Paint.
	COMMENTS	Generally low strength; tempered hardboard is strongest. Light weight. Available with a variety of factory-applied finishes.

Building a basic box

For stylish practicality, few storage containers surpass open, rectangular boxes. The simple lines of these versatile containers make them welcome in any room. Boxes can be stacked to form a handsome storage wall like the one at left, for records, books, stereo equipment and the like. Or they can be used singly to stow firewood, children's toys, Christmas ornaments and countless other refractory objects.

Best of all, a homemade box can be built to almost any dimensions, with a few caveats. Boxes generally are made of particleboard *(pages 72-73)*, to avoid the width limitations of solid lumber and the special edge finishes required by plywood. The one drawback to particleboard is its weight. In a suitably strong thickness of ¾ inch, particleboard weighs roughly 3 pounds per square foot; the 15-inch cube here weighs 20 pounds, and a 2-foot cube would weigh 60 pounds, the practical maximum for a single box. The sides of a rectangular box should not exceed 30 inches in length, lest they bend under heavy loads. And when designing stacked boxes, for maximum strength plan the joints so the horizontal pieces rest on the vertical ones and the screws that connect the pieces run vertically.

The construction of a box is as simple as its design. The sole difficulty is making perfectly straight cuts through an unwieldy sheet of particleboard. A lumberyard or a millwork dealer will do this job for a small fee; if you have a table saw, you can cut the pieces at home *(pages 120-121)*. Then use two corner clamps — ingenious tools that consist of a pair of small vises mounted at right angles — to align each joint while you fasten it with glue and screws. The completed box then can be spackled, sealed with shellac, sanded smooth and painted.

Materials List

Particleboard	1 piece ¾ " Eastern high-density particleboard, 4 ' x 4 ', cut into: 2 long sides, 15 " x 14¼ ", marked **A** and **C** 2 short sides, 13½ " x 14¼ ", marked **B** and **D** 1 back, 15 " x 15 ", marked **E**
Screws	24 No. 10 flat-head wood screws, 1½ " long
Glue	yellow carpenter's glue
Shellac	white shellac
Spackling compound	vinyl wall-patching compound
Paint	alkyd enamel

A basic box. Although this box is a perfect 15-inch cube, its pieces are of unequal dimensions to permit neat butt joints. Two long horizontal sides cover the ends of the short vertical sides, and the back covers all the rear edges. The pieces are joined with glue and screws. To forestall mistakes during assembly, each piece's outer face is marked with a handwritten letter — **A** and **C** aligned with the 15-inch edges, **B** and **D** aligned with the 13½-inch edges, **E** for the back.

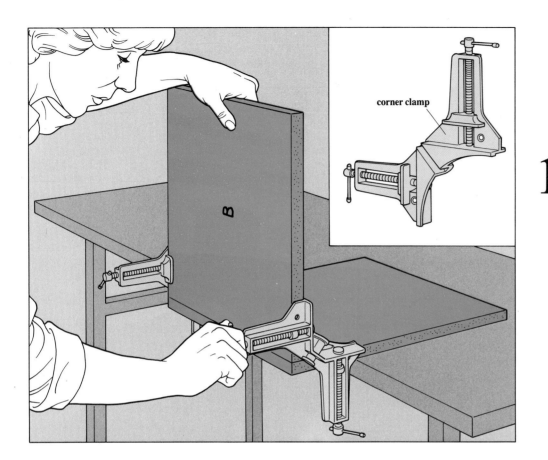

corner clamp

1 **Aligning a corner.** Set piece **A** flat on a table, with a short edge overhanging the table's edge. Tighten one leg of a corner clamp *(inset)* onto **A**, flush with the overhanging edge. Place piece **B** at a right angle to **A**, resting one of **B**'s long edges on **A**'s overhanging edge; arrange the pieces so that the letters are on their outer faces, with both letters reading correctly from the same vantage point and piece **B** to the right of **A**. Align **B**'s face flush with the overhanging edge, and secure **B** with the corner clamp; then install another corner clamp at the other end of the joint between **A** and **B**.

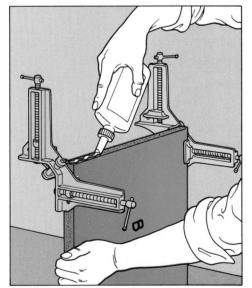

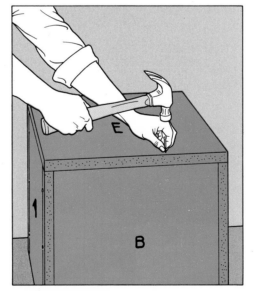

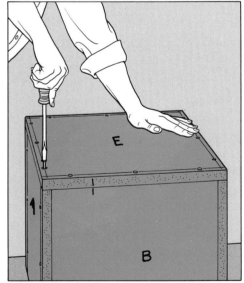

4 **Assembling the box.** Put corner clamps at each end of piece **B**'s left edge. Squeeze a ⅛-inch-wide glue bead across **B**'s end. Set **A**'s right edge over **B**'s glued end, and clamp **A** lightly. Drive 1½-inch No. 10 flat-head screws into the holes. Wipe away excess glue with a damp rag. Remove the corner clamps and repeat for pieces **C** and **D**, then attach the edges of **A** to **D** and **B** to **C**; proceed to Step 5 before the glue dries.

5 **Aligning the back.** Cover one of the box's open ends with piece **E**, and temporarily fasten it with two fourpenny nails, leaving the nailheads protruding. Drill three screw holes through each of **E**'s sides into the box edges *(Steps 2 and 3)*. Pencil a tick mark for future reference on one of **E**'s edges and on the adjacent side of the box. Then pull the nails with a claw hammer, placing a wood scrap beneath the hammer's head to protect **E**; proceed immediately to Step 6.

6 **Installing the back.** Apply a ⅛-inch-wide glue bead to the box's edges, align the tick marks on **E** and on the box, and fasten **E** to the box with 1½-inch No. 10 flat-head wood screws. Wipe away excess glue with a damp rag. After the glue has set overnight, smooth all rough edges with a sanding block fitted with medium (100-grit) paper.

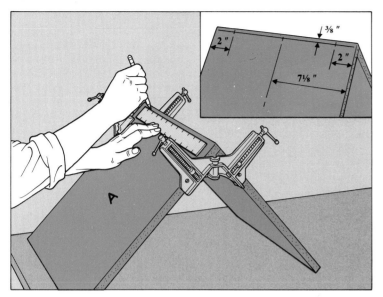

2 **Marking screw holes.** Set the assembly on a table with the clamped corner up. At the corner joint, measure ⅜ inch from the edge of piece **A** and draw a faint pencil line across the piece. Mark this line for screw holes in the middle and 2 inches from each end *(inset)*.

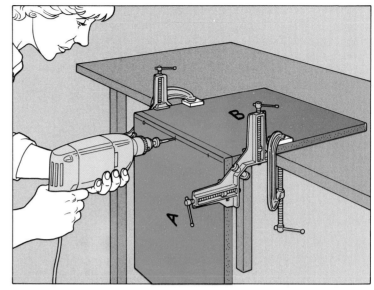

3 **Drilling the holes.** Use C clamps to secure piece **B** flat atop a workbench or a sturdy table, placing protective softwood scraps between **B** and the clamps. At each screw-hole mark, make counterbored pilot holes *(page 122)* for 1½-inch-long No. 10 wood screws, drilling horizontally through **A** into **B**'s end.

   Repeat Steps 1 through 3 for pieces **C** and **D**, adding each lettered piece in turn and drilling through the long pieces into the short ones.

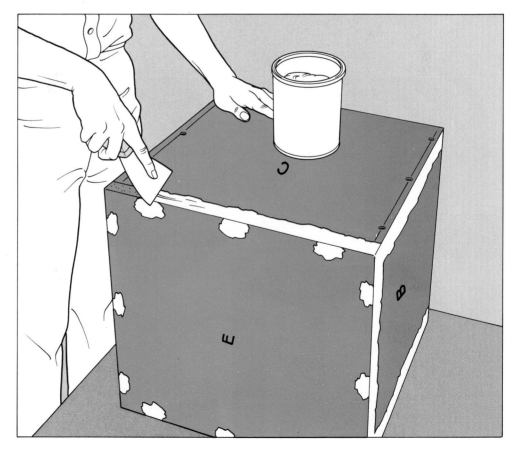

7 **Smoothing the surface.** With a putty knife, spread a thin layer of spackling compound along the box's edges and joints. Then push spackling compound into the counterbored holes with your finger, making a small mound over each screwhead. When the compound has cured, smooth it with a sanding block and fine (150-grit) paper.

Roll-away storage under a bed

The basic box, when built low and wide and mounted on casters, becomes a convenient storage unit that can be concealed beneath a bed. Handles attached to the front — one of the long edges — enable you to pull the box out and stow it again with ease.

A rollaway box can hold various household, recreational or clothing items: out-of-season jackets, for example, or lightweight athletic equipment such as tennis balls and racquets. It also makes an ideal toy chest for a child's room (below). If you use it to store sweaters, blankets, bed linens or extra pillows, cover them with a sheet of plastic to protect them from dust.

The box on these pages, designed to slip beneath a standard 39-inch-wide twin bed, measures 34 inches from front to back, 48 inches from side to side and 6½ inches top to base. Actual storage space inside the box is more than 4 cubic feet.

A box built for a double bed could measure up to 50 inches front to back. But a box more than 50 inches in any dimension would prove unwieldy, so for a queen- or king-sized bed, build two smaller boxes and put them under the bed back-to-back. The box shown is 7 inches high mounted on its casters — shallow enough to slide under most beds. If you have a higher bed, you may want to build a deeper box.

This particular box is constructed of birch hardwood plywood graded A2 (page 72). Make sure the A (premium) surface of the wood is employed in the most visible positions. For instance, the A side of the bottom panel should face up while the lower quality surface, rated 2, is turned toward the floor. The A side of the front panel should face the front; the premium side of the back and side panels should face outward.

All of the pieces required can be sawed from a single 4-by-8-foot plywood sheet. You can cut the pieces yourself (pages 119-121). Or you can buy the plywood at a lumberyard that will saw it for you. Tell the dealer what the wood is for and that the cuts must be precise so the pieces will fit together squarely in butt joints.

Spherical steel casters of the type used here (Materials List, opposite) are available at most hardware stores. They should have metal treads if the box will be on a carpeted floor; resilient rubber or plastic treads are best for bare floors.

Choose generously sized handles that are fixed by screws long enough to pass all the way through the front panel of the box. Handles attached only by screws driven into the face of the wood might come loose with continued use.

To hold pieces in place while you work, you will need two C clamps and two corner clamps (page 76). You may want to have a helper to steady components while you are clamping them into position — especially if you have previously applied glue to the pieces.

You will also need an adjustable counterbore bit, or bits that will drill counterbored pilot holes for No. 10 screws (page 122), as well as simple twist bits.

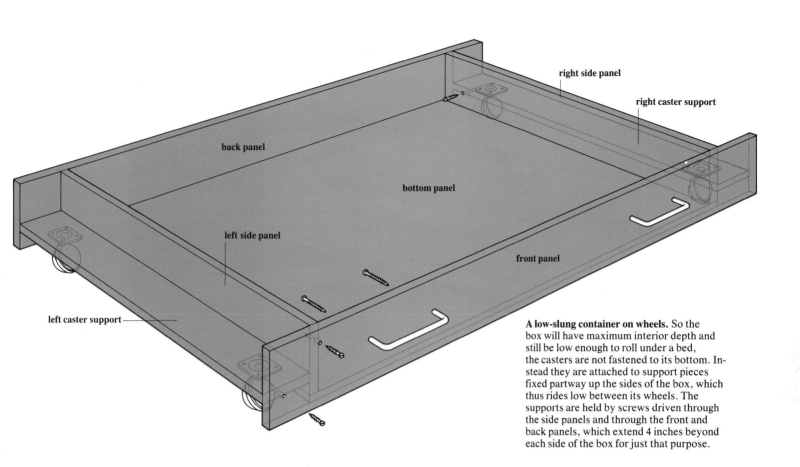

right side panel

right caster support

back panel

bottom panel

left side panel

front panel

left caster support

A low-slung container on wheels. So the box will have maximum interior depth and still be low enough to roll under a bed, the casters are not fastened to its bottom. Instead they are attached to support pieces fixed partway up the sides of the box, which thus rides low between its wheels. The supports are held by screws driven through the side panels and through the front and back panels, which extend 4 inches beyond each side of the box for just that purpose.

Materials List

Plywood	1 sheet A2-quality ¾ ″ hardwood plywood, 4 ′ x 8 ′, cut into: 2 side panels, each 32½ ″ x 5¾ ″ 2 caster supports, each 32½ ″ x 4 ″ 1 front panel and 1 back panel, each 48 ″ x 6½ ″ 1 bottom panel 32½ ″ x 40 ″
Casters	4 casters with 2 ″ wheels, plastic treads, flat steel plates, and a rated load capacity of 75 lbs. per caster
Handles	2 drawer handles with threaded shanks
Screws	50 No. 10 flat-head wood screws, 1½ ″ long 16 No. 6 flat-head wood screws, ⅝ ″ long
Fillers	spackling compound and wood putty
Glue	yellow carpenter's glue
Paint	acrylic primer and semigloss acrylic paint

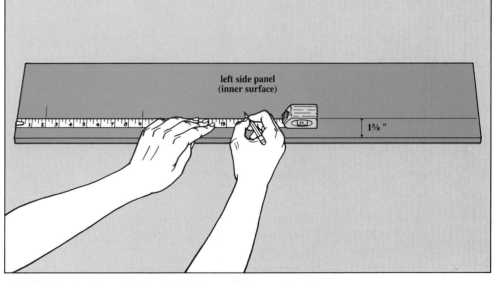

left side panel
(inner surface)

1⅝ ″

1 **Marking the side panels.** On the left side panel's inner surface, draw a line 1⅝ inches from the lower edge. Make five short pencil marks across the line: 2 inches and 9 inches from each end and at the board's center. These marks designate the positions for screws that will hold the caster support to the side panel. Then turn the board over and draw a line 2 inches from the lower edge on the outer surface; this line will guide you in positioning the caster support. Now draw identical lines and marks on the inner and outer surfaces of the right side panel.▶

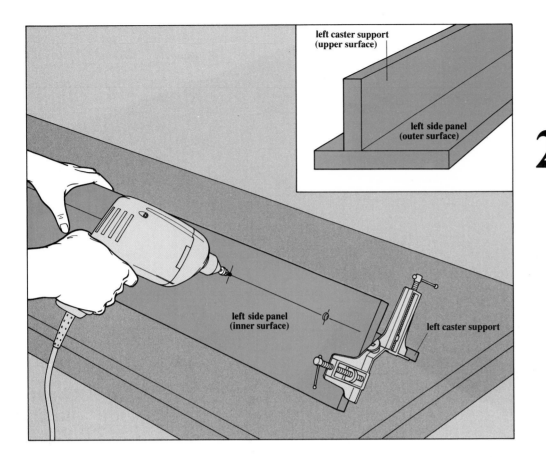

left caster support
(upper surface)

left side panel
(outer surface)

left side panel
(inner surface)

left caster support

2 **Drilling pilot holes in the side pieces.** Lay the left side panel on the worktable, outer surface upward. Stand the left caster support on edge on top of the panel. Put the two pieces together, aligning what will be the upper surface of the support with the penciled line on the side panel *(inset);* fix them with corner clamps. Now turn the clamped assemblage over to reveal the inner surface of the side panel with its marked screw-hole positions. Drill 1½-inch-deep counterbored holes for No. 10 screws at the marks, through the side panel and into the caster support. Unclamp the pieces, clamp the right side panel and the right caster support together in the same way, and drill the pilot holes in those pieces.

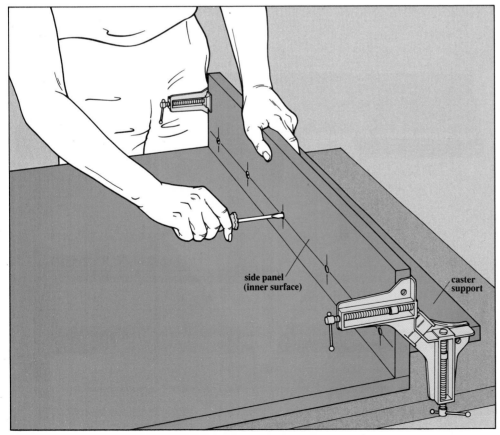

side panel
(inner surface)

caster
support

5 **Attaching the caster supports.** Squeeze a line of glue along the inner edge of the left caster support. Clamp the support to the outer surface of the left side panel, using the pencil line to position it as you did in Step 2. Now drive 1½-inch No. 10 flat-head wood screws into the counterbored holes. Remove the clamps, then attach the right caster support to the right side panel similarly.

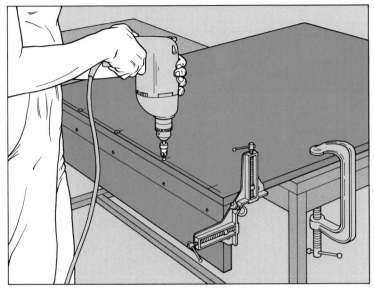

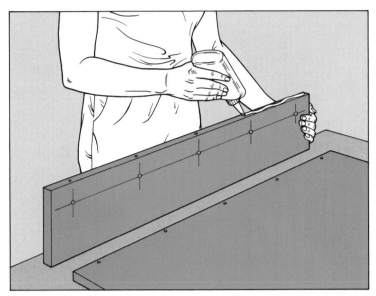

3 **Putting screw holes in the bottom panel.** Lay the bottom panel on a worktable with its lower-quality underside facing up. Clamp one long edge to the table. Draw a line ⅜ inch from each of the shorter, side edges to mark the position of the center of the edge of each side panel. Make five ticks across each line: 2 inches and 9 inches from the ends of the bottom panel and at the center. Now use corner clamps to affix the left side panel upside down, with its outer surface facing outward and flush with the bottom panel's side edge. Drill 1½-inch-deep counterbored holes through the bottom panel and into the side panel at the marked locations. Remove that panel, clamp the right side panel to the other side edge of the bottom piece, and drill the holes marked along that side.

4 **Fixing the side panels to the bottom.** Turn the bottom panel over so that its good side faces upward. Hold the left side panel upside down and run a line of glue along what will be its lower edge. Turn the side panel over, position it so its outer surface is flush with the left edge of the bottom panel and press it into place. Clamp the pieces together with the corner clamps. Use a damp cloth to wipe away any glue that squeezes out of the joint. From underneath, drive 1½-inch No. 10 flat-head wood screws into the holes you drilled in Step 3. Then remove the clamps, and use them to hold the right side panel in place as you glue and screw it to the right edge of the bottom panel.

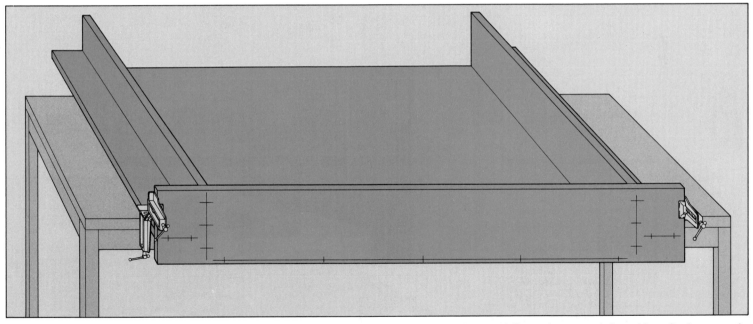

6 **Marking the front panel for screw holes.** Clamp the front panel to the caster supports *(above)*. Draw vertical lines centered on the front panel where the ends of the side panels butt against it; then draw a horizontal line ⅜ inch from the lower edge of the front panel, and shorter horizontal lines centered along the ends of the caster supports. Now make cross marks on each line to show screw-hole positions: On the two vertical lines, mark at 1 inch, 3 inches and 5 inches from the top of the front panel; on the long horizontal line, mark 6 inches and 15 inches from each end and at the center of the front panel; on the short horizontal lines, make cross marks 1 inch and 3 inches from the outer ends.▶

7 **Drilling pilot holes through the front and back panels.** Drill 1½-inch-deep counterbored holes for No. 10 screws at each penciled location on the front panel. Remove the front panel, and clamp the back panel to the other side of the box. Mark it with lines and screw locations identical to those you penciled on the front panel, in Step 6. Drill pilot holes at those places and remove the clamps.

8 **Fastening the front and back panels.** Stand the box on its back edges on the floor. Squeeze glue onto the upward-facing edges. Put the front panel in place — the same position it occupied in Steps 6 and 7 — and clamp it. Wipe away excess glue with a damp cloth. Drive 1½-inch No. 10 flat-head wood screws into the counterbored holes. Now remove the clamps, turn the box over so that it rests on the front panel, and attach the back panel the same way. Lay the box flat, spread spackling compound onto all the exposed plywood edges *(page 77, Step 7),* and cover the visible screwheads with wood putty, slightly overfilling the holes. Let the glue and fillers dry for 24 hours, then sand the edges and other filled places smooth with fine (150-grit) sandpaper.

10 **Drilling holes for the handles.** Draw a line the length of the front panel, midway between the top and bottom edges. Pencil light marks 12 inches from each end. Then measure the distance between the centers of the holes in a handle, and mark off that distance toward the middle of the panel from each of the first marks *(right).* To keep the plywood from splintering when you drill through it, clamp a piece of scrap wood to the back of the panel behind one pair of marks (use a smaller scrap under the top jaw of the C clamp to protect the panel's face). With a bit slightly larger in diameter than your handles' screws, drill those two holes, then move the clamp and scrap wood, and drill the other pair of holes.

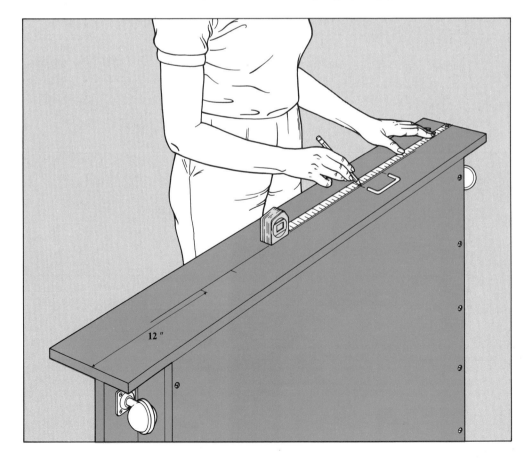

9 **Attaching the casters.** Turn the box upside down on the worktable. At each corner, draw lines on the bottom of the caster support as seen at right — one line 3 inches from the side panel, and an intersecting line 3 inches from the adjacent panel. Position a caster within the corner formed by the two lines, and pencil the outlines of its screw holes onto the caster support. Using a 3/32-inch twist bit, drill a pilot hole 5/8 inch deep at each mark; to make sure you do not bore all the way through the plywood, mark the bit with a band of masking tape 5/8 of an inch from the tip and stop drilling when the tape touches the surface of the wood. Attach the caster using 5/8-inch No. 6 flat-head wood screws. Fix the other casters to the box the same way.

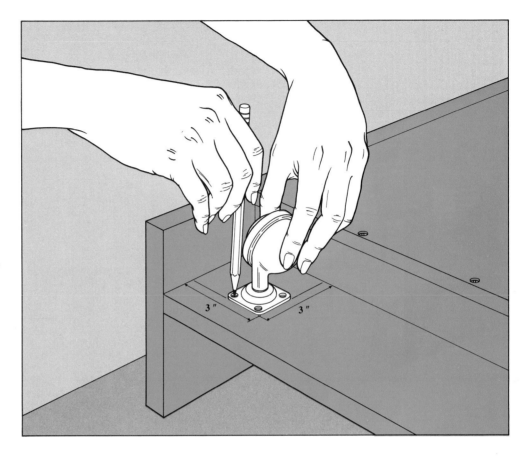

11 **Finishing the job.** Lightly sand all the box's visible surfaces with fine (150-grit) sandpaper, and paint the box. After the paint has dried, slip a handle screw through a hole in the front panel and start turning it into one of the threaded holes in a handle by hand. Before tightening that screw, insert the screw for the other end of the handle and start turning it by hand. Then tighten both screws with a screwdriver *(right)*. Attach the other handle the same way.

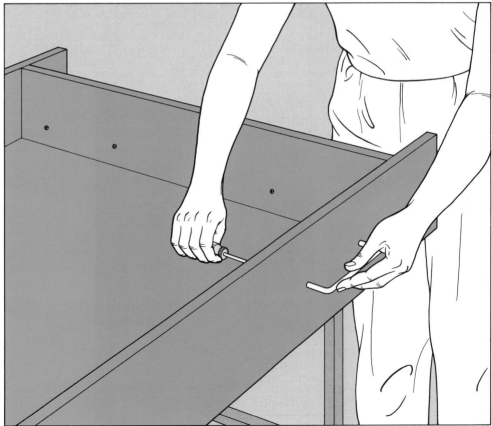

Capacious bins that fit below stairs

Putting space under the stairway to the best use requires movable units such as the graduated storage bins shown below. They roll out on concealed casters to give full access to their contents, then roll back under the stairway to hide behind a smooth façade. A small, nonmoving filler covers the tip of the angle between stairs and floor in front of the bins.

The bins shown here contain cleaning supplies and are outfitted accordingly with hooks and clips screwed to furring strips. Alternatively, you might use the space for toys, sports equipment or hobby paraphernalia — after putting appropriate hangers or dividers inside the bins.

Fundamentally, the bins are just boxes with their tops shaped to match the angle of the stairs. Getting the angle of the slope

right depends on making one cardboard template to serve as a guide for marking and cutting the side panels of both bins. The width of the side panels can vary with the length of the available space under the stairs. Here, the panels are 23¾ inches wide so two will fit next to each other on a 4-by-8-foot sheet of plywood.

The depth of the space under the stairs governs the depth of the bins. Measure

the distance from the wall to the outside of the stairs, then plan the bins with a depth about 2 inches less than this measurement. This ensures that when the bins are rolled under the stairs, the angled side panels will be recessed behind the diagonal stair stringer.

If you plan to paint the bins, you can make them entirely from construction-grade plywood. If the exposed panels are to receive a natural finish, these should be made from hardwood plywood, but the other panels can be made from construction grade. With a circular saw, you can do the cutting yourself *(pages 118-119),* taking particular care with the diagonal cuts. Otherwise, take your template to a lumberyard, mark the plywood and have it sawed there.

After the bins are built you will need to measure them to determine the exact lengths of furring strip and molding you will need *(right);* the figures in the Materials List suit the bins shown here. You will need casters, handles, and hooks or clips for securing the contents. Choose spherical casters *(page 83)* to make it easy to roll the loaded bins in any direction. The handles should be large enough to provide you with a good grip, and styled to fit in with the rest of the room. Select the variety of hooks and clips that will keep the contents of the bins neatly in their places.

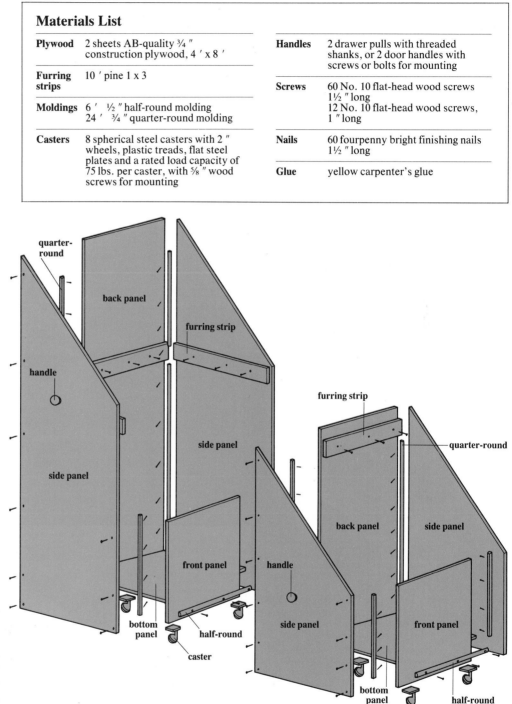

Materials List

Plywood	2 sheets AB-quality ¾ ″ construction plywood, 4 ′ x 8 ′		**Handles**	2 drawer pulls with threaded shanks, or 2 door handles with screws or bolts for mounting
Furring strips	10 ′ pine 1 x 3		**Screws**	60 No. 10 flat-head wood screws 1½ ″ long 12 No. 10 flat-head wood screws, 1 ″ long
Moldings	6 ′ ½ ″ half-round molding 24 ′ ¾ ″ quarter-round molding		**Nails**	60 fourpenny bright finishing nails 1½ ″ long
Casters	8 spherical steel casters with 2 ″ wheels, plastic treads, flat steel plates and a rated load capacity of 75 lbs. per caster, with ⅝ ″ wood screws for mounting		**Glue**	yellow carpenter's glue

Rolling bins. The front, back, bottom and side panels of the bins are ¾-inch plywood and are held together by glue and flat-head wood screws. Quarter-round molding reinforces inside corners; half-round molding forms bumper strips to maintain clearance between the bins. Lengths of furring strip are screwed to the vertical panels to provide a solid base for attaching hooks and spring clips. Spherical casters, hidden behind the overhanging vertical panels, allow the bins to roll in any direction.

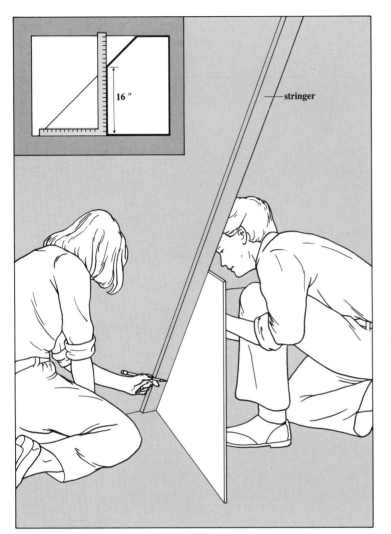

1 Producing a template for side panels. With a straightedge and a sharp utility knife, cut a perfectly straight edge on a large piece of cardboard. Set this cut edge on the floor so that the cardboard covers the opening where the stairs and floor meet. While a helper holds the cardboard, run a pencil along the bottom of the stair stringer to trace the angle of the stairs onto the cardboard *(above)*. Lay the cardboard on a flat work surface, and use the straightedge and pencil to straighten the line. Align the outer edge of one leg of a carpenter's square with the straight bottom edge of the cardboard; then draw a line perpendicular to the bottom at the point where the diagonal is 16 inches above it *(inset)*. Use the straightedge and utility knife to cut along this line, and then along the diagonal line to finish the template.

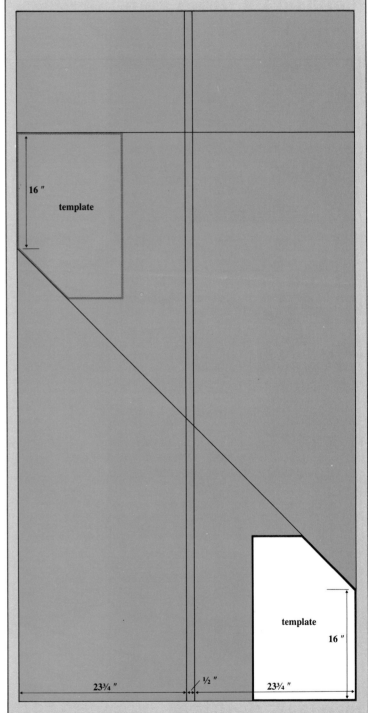

2 Marking and cutting the side panels. Align the template with one corner of a sheet of plywood, setting the 16-inch edge along one long side of the plywood. Use the template's diagonal edge as a guide to pencil a line on the plywood; use a straight board as a guide for extending this line to the opposite side of the sheet. Move the template across the sheet, and set the diagonal edge on the pencil line and the 16-inch edge along the long side of the sheet. Make a mark on the edge of the plywood at the 90° corner of the template. Then draw a line from this mark, perpendicular to the edge, all the way across the sheet. Next draw lines 23¾ inches from each long edge. Use a circular saw and straightedge guide *(page 119)* to cut the plywood sheet along all the marked lines.

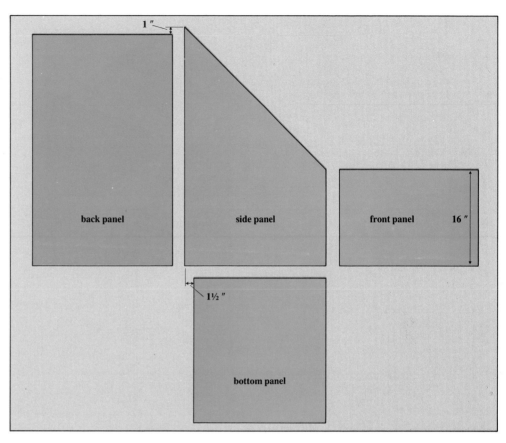

3 **Cutting the other panels.** To determine the depth for the bins, measure from the outside edge of the stair stringer to a point 2 inches from the wall. Then measure, mark and cut two sets of front, back and bottom panels. Make each front panel 16 inches high; its width should be 1½ inches less than the depth of the bin, to allow for the thickness of the side panels. Each back panel is 1 inch shorter than the long edge of its side panel, and the same width as the front panel. Each bottom panel is 1½ inches shorter than the width of the side panel, and the same width as the front and back panels.

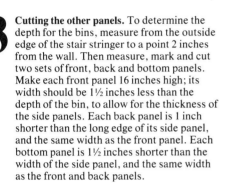

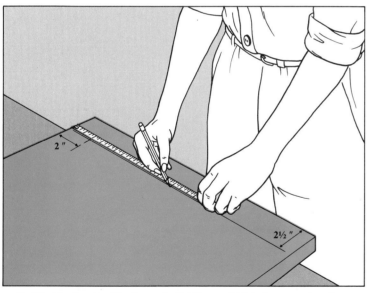

4 **Marking front and back panels.** Put the small bin's front panel on the worktable with its inner side up. Draw a line across the panel 2⅛ inches from the bottom edge, to indicate the position of the lower face of the bottom panel when the bin is assembled. Turn the front panel over, draw a line 2½ inches from the bottom edge *(above),* and mark screw-hole positions 2 inches from each end of the line and in the center. Mark lines and screw-hole positions on the back panel in the same way, then mark the front and back panels of the large bin.

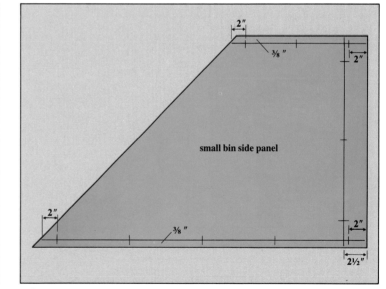

5 **Marking side panels.** On the outer face of a side panel for the small bin, draw a line ⅜ inch from the long edge. Mark screw-hole positions 2 inches from each end of the line and at three equal intervals between the end marks. On a similar line parallel to the short edge, mark screw-hole positions 2 inches from each end and in the center. Draw a line 2½ inches from the bottom edge; mark screw-hole positions 2 inches from each end and in the center. Mark the opposite side panel similarly.

Mark the side panels of the large bin in the same way, but with seven screw-hole positions along the long edge. ▶

87

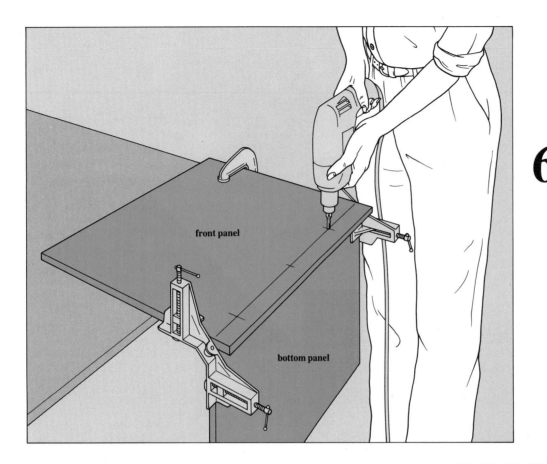

6 **Drilling front and back panels.** Use corner clamps to secure the bottom panel of the small bin to the front panel, setting the lower face of the bottom panel flush with the line you drew 2⅛ inches from the bottom of the front panel. Drill counterbored holes for 1½-inch No. 10 screws through the three marked points on the front panel, into the bottom panel. Drive screws into each of the end holes, then remove the clamps. Clamp the opposite edge of the bottom to the back panel of the small bin in the same way, and drill screw-holes at the marked positions. Drive screws into the two end holes and remove the clamps.

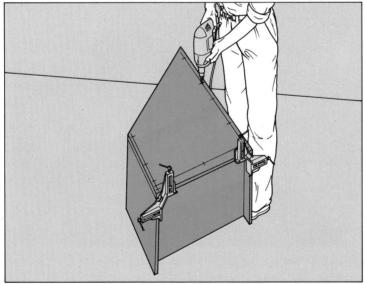

8 **Drilling the side panel.** Drill counterbored holes for 1½-inch No. 10 screws through the marked positions on the side panel, into the edges of the back, front and bottom panels. Drive screws into the top and bottom holes of the front and back edges of the side panel, then remove the corner clamps from the assembly.

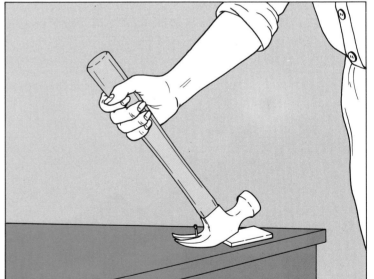

9 **Putting on the second side.** Using a claw hammer with a piece of scrap wood underneath to protect the surface, pull the nails that held the side panel while you drilled it. Drill screw holes through the nail holes. Turn the assembly over and repeat Steps 7 and 8 to drill holes in the other side panel. Mark the bottom face and front edge of the bottom panel so you can identify them later, then remove all the screws from the assembly. Reassemble the bin in the sequence shown in Steps 6, 7 and 8, applying glue to each joined edge before screwing it into place. Starting with Step 6, repeat the entire procedure to assemble the large bin.

7 **Nailing a side panel.** Lay the assembly on the floor with the front, back and bottom panels on edge. Use corner clamps to secure the matching side panel so that its bottom edge is flush with the bottom edges of the front and back panels and the face with marked screw holes is facing up.

Align the long edge of the side panel with the outer face of the back panel. To secure the side panel to the back panel, drive a sixpenny (2-inch) nail through the screwhole position nearest the top of the side panel. Leave the nailhead protruding so you can remove it later. Secure the short edge of the side panel to the front panel similarly.

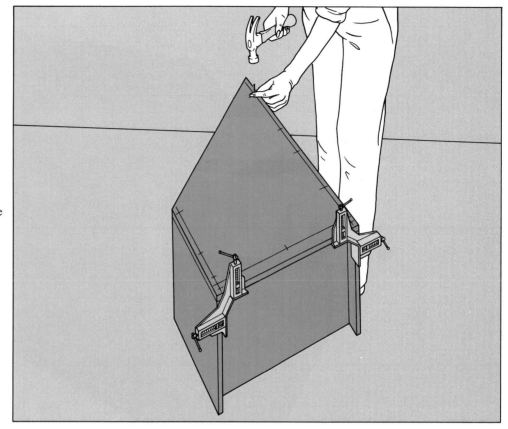

10 **Attaching furring strips.** Cut a piece of 1-by-3 as long as the width of the back panel. Position it inside the small bin, parallel to the top edge of the back panel and 1 inch from that edge. Tack it into place with two small nails, leaving the heads protruding for easy removal. Drill counterbored holes for three 1 ″ No. 10 screws near the ends and in the center of the furring strip; be careful not to drill too deep, going through the back panel.

Pull out the nails, coat the furring strip with glue, and screw it into place. Use the same technique to fasten furring strips to the back and sides of the large bin, one inch lower than the top of the short edge of the side panel. ▶

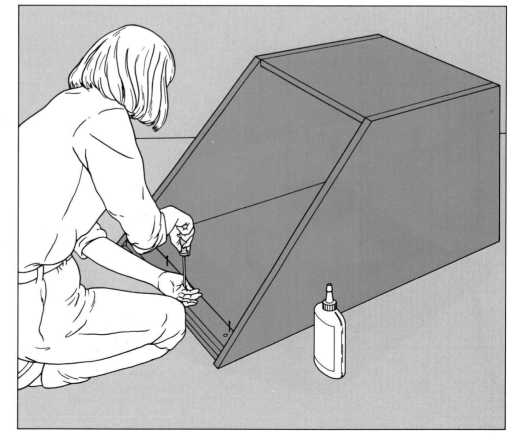

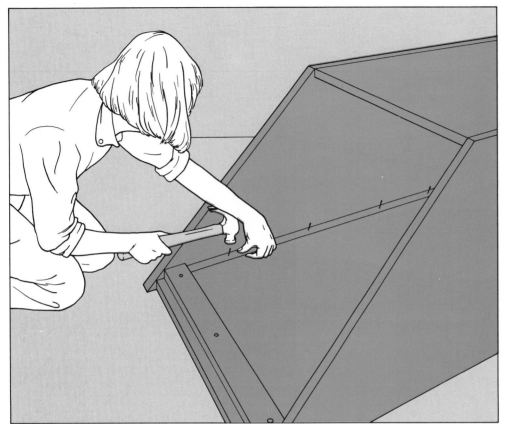

11 **Reinforcing the corners.** Measure the distance from the floor of the small bin to the bottom of the furring strip, then cut two pieces of ¾-inch quarter-round molding to this length. Cut two other pieces of quarter-round molding as long as the distance from the floor of the bin to the top edge of the front panel. Drive fourpenny (1½-inch) finishing nails through the rounded sides of the molding at 6-inch intervals so the points of the nails are just visible through the angle opposite. Coat the flat edges of the strips with glue, and nail them into the corners of the bin. Repeat the process for the corners of the large bin.

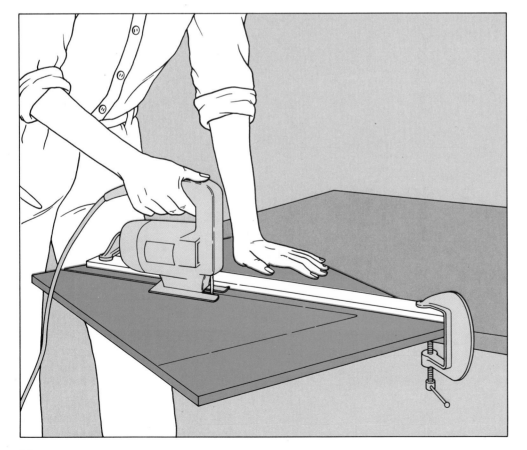

13 **Cutting sides for the filler.** Roll the small bin under the stairs so its angled top is ½ inch below the stringer. Make a pencil mark on the floor ½ inch from the forward edge of the front panel. Take a piece of plywood with two straight edges meeting in a square corner, and hold it over the opening beneath the stairs with the square corner on the pencil mark. Trace on the plywood the shape of the intersection between the stringer and the floor. Clamp the plywood to the edge of the worktable and use a saber saw to cut the shape of the short end, then use a guide with the saber saw or a circular saw to cut the diagonal edge. Use this piece as a template for marking and cutting an identical piece.

12 **Attaching bumper strips.** Cut a length of ½-inch half-round molding as long as the depth of the small bin. Drive fourpenny finishing nails into the rounded side at intervals of 6 to 8 inches, hammering them only far enough to make their points emerge from the flat side. Apply glue to the flat side of the molding, align it with the bottom edge of the front of the bin, and nail it into place. Cut, glue and nail an identical piece to the bottom front of the large bin. Attach casters at each corner of the bottom, following the instructions on page 83, Step 9.

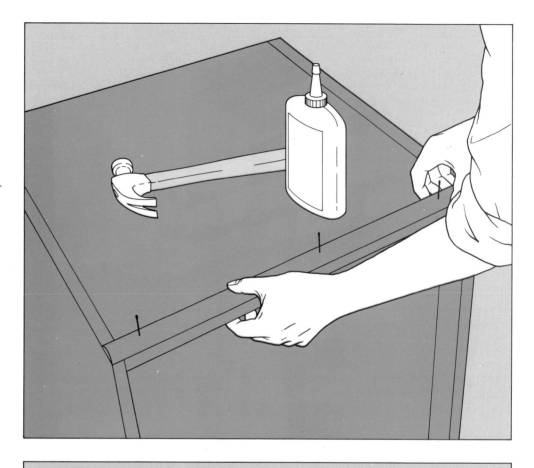

14 **Assembling the filler.** For the filler, cut a rectangular back panel that is 1½ inches shorter than the depth of the bins, and about 1 inch lower than the long edge of the filler's side panels. Cut a 1-by-3 brace 1½ inches shorter than the depth of the bins. Assemble the pieces as shown at right, using glue and countersunk 1½-inch No. 10 screws. Finish the filler, and the two bins, by spackling the exposed edges, filling nail and screw holes, sanding and painting. Install handles *(page 83, Step 11)* in the center of the outer side panel of each bin.

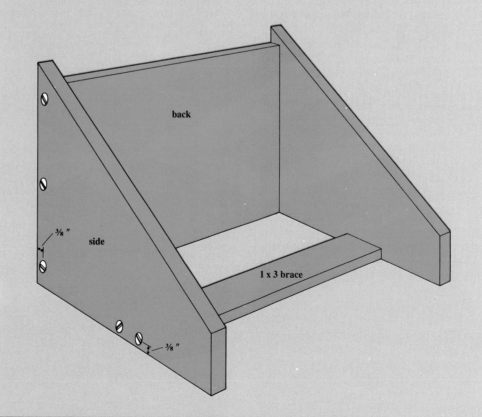

back

⅜ "

side

1 x 3 brace

⅜ "

A slatted storage bench for outdoor gear

Slickers, galoshes, snowsuits, ski boots and umbrellas — all of the family's winter and foul-weather gear — should receive special treatment when icy, wet or muddy. The ingenious bin at right provides just that. Closed, the bin forms a handy seat to use while removing wet footwear, which then goes inside the bin. A well at the bin's back accommodates umbrellas and skis. Coats and ski poles hang from the peg rack, built as described on pages 46-47 and mounted on the wall behind the bin. All of this sodden impedimenta drips into plastic trays beneath the bin, and the footwear inside dries in air that circulates through gaps between the bin's slats.

The bin demonstrated here is 16¼ inches high. It measures 43 inches from side to side and 24 inches from front to back — dimensions suited to a pair of 16-by-20-inch photographic developing trays underneath, but easily modified for other shallow drip pans. The boards — 1-by-4s and a few 1-by-2s — can be cut to length at a lumberyard or millwork. Or you can do the job at home with a table saw or a circular saw *(pages 119-121),* or even with a miter box and sharp backsaw.

The key to building the bin is to join the various pieces squarely, at perfect right angles. This requires making a dry run by first temporarily fastening the rectangular frames for the sides with one screw at each corner and adjusting the joints until the frame is square, then securing each joint with a second screw. During this procedure you should barely tighten each screw, lest you strip its pilot hole. When all the pieces are aligned, the entire bin is disassembled so the joints can be glued and fastened permanently with screws.

The bin's hardware has two components, available at builder's-hardware stores. The lid is mounted on a continuous hinge (often called a piano hinge), which can be cut to length with a hacksaw. The lid's descent is cushioned by a piston-action pneumatic brake, a safety device that keeps the lid from slamming on a hand or, worse, a head or shoulders.

To waterproof the boards, sand the bin inside and out with fine (150-grit) paper; then brush on a clear, penetrating, water-resistant finish, such as one used on gymnasium floors. Apply at least one additional coat of the penetrating finish, sanding between coats, then complete the job with a coat of paste wax.

Materials List

1 x 4	80 ′ clear pine 1 x 4, cut into:
	5 top pieces, 44½ ″ long 6 front and back pieces, 43 ″ long 1 hinge brace, 41½ ″ long 8 side pieces, 22½ ″ long 3 lid braces, 13¾ ″ long 4 corner braces and 2 bottom braces, 15½ ″ long
1 x 2	24 ′ clear pine 1 x 2, cut into:
	5 bottom slats, 41½ ″ long 1 center brace, 19 ″ long
Hinge	1 continuous hinge, 48 ″ long, 1½ ″ wide, with screws
Screws	130 No. 10 flat-head wood screws, 1½ ″ long 4 No. 10 flat-head wood screws, 2 ″ long
Lid support	pneumatic lid support
Glue	yellow carpenter's glue
Finish	clear, penetrating, water-resistant finish; paste wax
Trays	2 photographic developing trays, 16 ″ x 20 ″

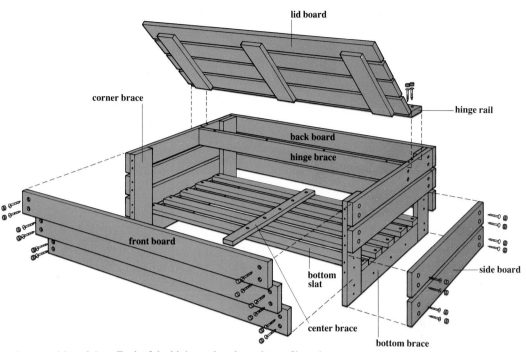

A composition of slats. Each of the bin's sections is made up of boards glued and screwed to an underlying brace, a technique that reinforces the structure and avoids split ends. The sides are four boards tall, but the front and back panels lack a bottom board, leaving space for plastic drip pans. At the bin's back, a hinge brace and a hinge rail separate the lid from a deep well for skis and umbrellas. The lid is mounted on the hinge rail with a continuous hinge; a pneumatic lid support (*not shown*) holds the lid open and eases its closing.

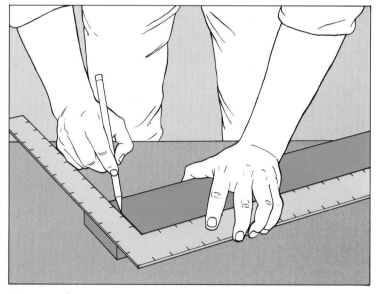

1 **Marking the screw holes.** Align a carpenter's square with one end of a 22½-inch 1-by-4, placing the square's 1½-inch-wide shorter leg, or tongue, over the board's end. Draw a line along the tongue, then mark across the line for screw holes 1 inch from each edge of the board. Mark screw holes similarly on the other end of the board, then on both ends of the seven remaining side pieces. Resting each board on a wood scrap, drill counterbored shank holes (*page 122*) for No. 10 screws at the marks, with the counterbore extending about ¼ inch below the surface.

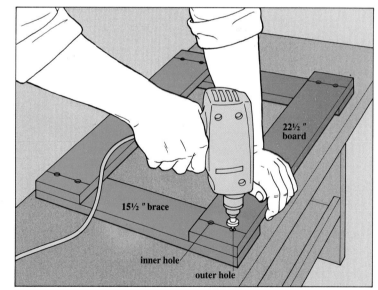

2 **Drilling pilot holes.** To assemble the frame for one of the box's sides, set two 15½-inch-long 1-by-4 braces parallel on a worktable, and rest two 22½-inch boards from Step 1 on top of them. Adjust the boards until each is at right angles to the braces, its ends flush with their edges. Then at each corner slide a pilot-hole bit for No. 10 screws through the outer hole from Step 1, and drill about halfway through the 15½-inch brace. Do not yet drill a pilot hole through the inner hole.▶

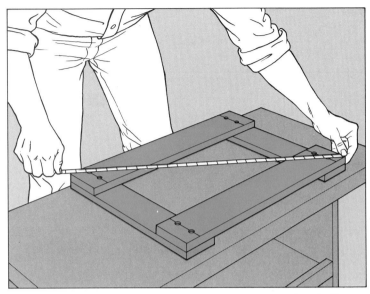

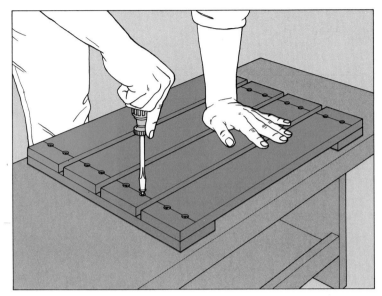

3 **Squaring the frame.** Drive a 1½-inch No. 10 screw through each pilot hole from Step 2. Then compare the frame's two diagonal measurements, and pivot the boards until the diagonals are exactly the same length. At each corner, drill a pilot hole into the brace beneath the unfilled shank hole from Step 1, and fasten the boards with another No. 10 screw.

4 **Completing the side.** Set two already-drilled 22½-inch boards from Step 1 within the rectangular frame, leaving even gaps between boards. Mark the position of each board, then hold it down firmly and drill pilot holes through the predrilled holes into the underlying brace. Drive a 1½-inch-long No. 10 screw through each hole. Assemble the other side of the box by repeating Steps 2 through 4.

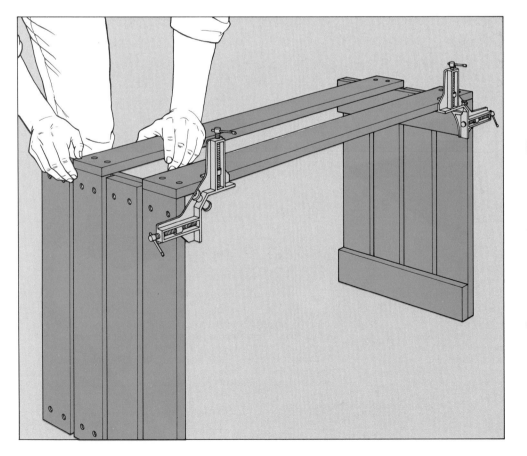

6 **Completing the back.** Set another 43-inch board across the side panels, one board away from their unfastened corners, to leave room for the drip pans. At each end, drill one pilot hole through the predrilled shank holes into the brace, and fasten the board with 1½-inch No. 10 screws. Remove the corner clamps. Square the back as in Step 3, then drive No. 10 screws through the unfilled shank holes into the braces. Fasten a third 43-inch board similarly between the other two. Invert the resulting three-sided assembly and add the final side of the box by repeating Steps 5 and 6.

7 **Labeling the parts.** Mark each board so that you will be able to reassemble the box properly: Set the rack upright and write consecutive numbers on the end of each corner brace. To minimize marking the face of the box, write the same number on the inside of each board end that is screwed to the brace. On each side of the box, letter the inner face of each board, working down in layers from the top. Then unscrew each board and disassemble the entire box.▶

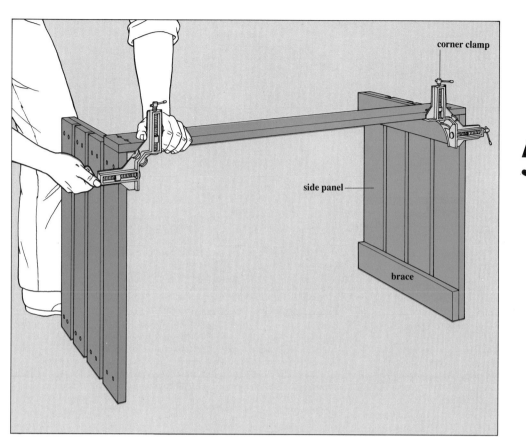

corner clamp

side panel

brace

5 **Joining the sides.** On all six 43-inch boards, draw a line 1⅛ inch from each end, and mark across it for screw holes 1 inch from each edge. At each mark, drill counterbored shank holes for No. 10 screws. Stand the side panels from Step 4 on their ends on the floor, with their 15½-inch-long braces running horizontally and facing each other. Set a 43-inch board atop the side panels, aligning its ends with their corners, and secure each end with a corner clamp *(page 76, Step 1, inset)*. Drill a pilot hole at each end through the outer shank hole into the brace, and fasten the boards with No. 10 screws 1½ inches long.

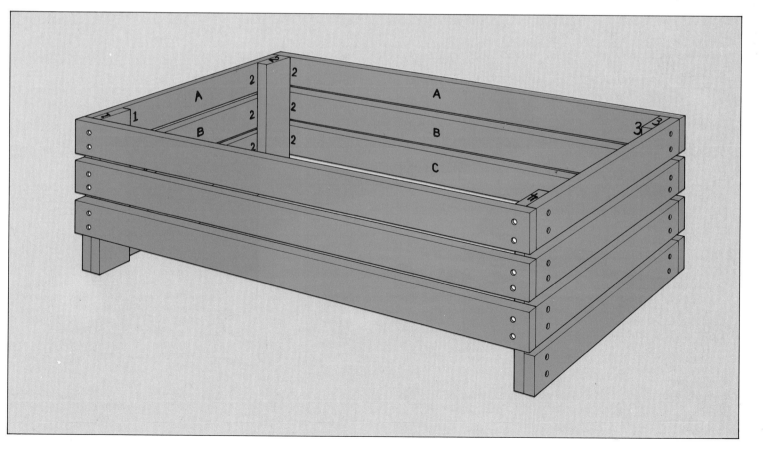

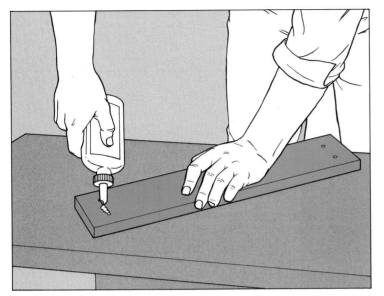

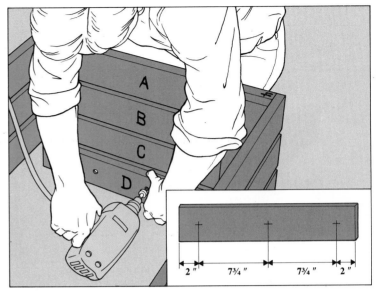

8 **Gluing the box.** Using a sanding block and medium (100-grit) sandpaper, smooth the back of each screw hole and the sharp edges of each board. Glue the box together, following the sequence in Steps 2 through 6: Squeeze a ⅛-inch-wide line of glue between the screw holes at each end of a 22½-inch board marked **A** and fasten the board to its braces, then similarly glue and fasten the matching bottom board, marked **D**, and the intervening boards. Assemble the other side panel, then join the side panels with the 43-inch boards for the front and back.

9 **Installing the bottom braces.** Along the center of a 15½-inch board, mark for screw holes in the middle of the board and 2 inches from each end *(inset);* then drill counterbored shank holes for 1½-inch No. 10 screws at each mark. Sand away any splinters behind the holes. Rest the bottom brace on the floor between one pair of corner braces, flush with the bottom board of a side panel, and drill pilot holes for the screws through the shank holes into the bottom board. Apply a ⅛-inch-wide line of glue along the center of the brace, and screw the brace to the bottom board. Fasten another brace to the box's other side panel.

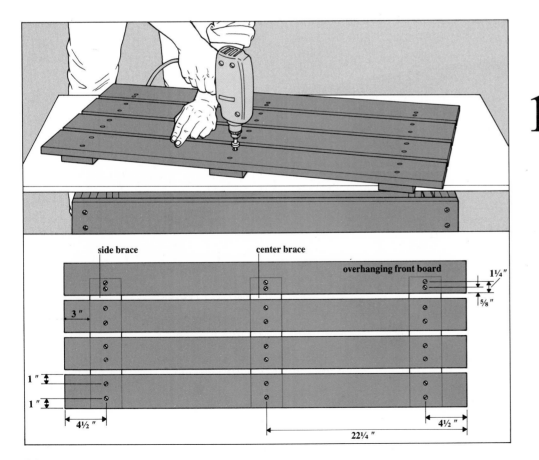

12 **Making the lid.** On each of three 44½-inch boards, drill pairs of counterbored shank holes for 1½-inch No. 10 screws, 1 inch in from each edge, in the middle of the board and 4½ inches from each end. Mark a fourth board for the lid's overhanging front in the same way, but place the holes ⅝ inch and 1¼ inches from one edge. Set a predrilled board squarely across the ends of two 13¾-inch side braces. Place each brace's outer edge 3 inches from the board's end; then drill one pilot hole at each joint, and screw the parts together. Align the predrilled front board similarly, with its outer edge 15½ inches from the lid's back, and drive one screw into each end. Square and fasten the resulting rectangle *(Step 3)*, then screw the two remaining boards between the outer ones. Secure each board to a 13¾-inch center brace through the remaining shank holes.

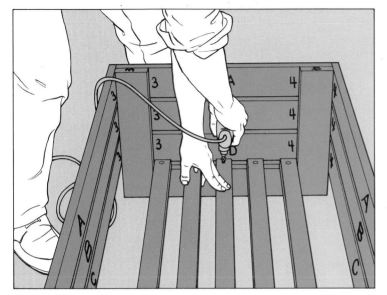

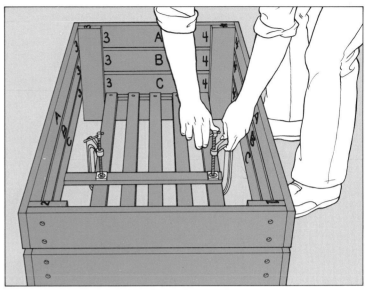

10 **Adding bottom slats.** On the center line of each of five 1-by-2 slats, mark for screw holes in the middle and ⅜ inch from each end. Drill counterbored shank holes for 1½-inch No. 10 screws at the marks. Put a slat flat on the bottom braces, tightly against opposing corner braces. Drill pilot holes through the shank holes into the bottom braces, and fasten the slat with screws; no glue is needed. Fasten another slat similarly at the opposite side of the box, then space the remaining slats evenly between the outer two.

11 **Attaching the center brace.** To keep water from dripping between the pans, center a 19-inch 1-by-2 on the slats and secure it with C clamps, its front end overhanging the front slat as shown. Drill one counterbored shank hole and one pilot hole at each slat, and fasten the 1-by-2 with 1½-inch No. 10 screws.

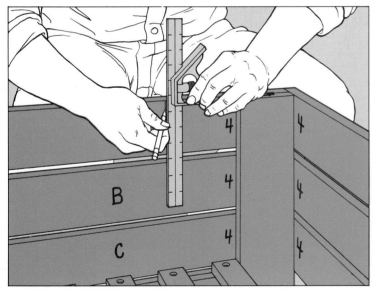

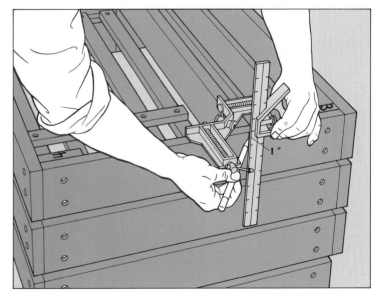

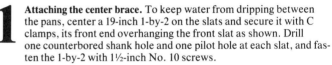

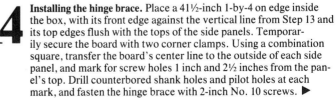

13 **Aligning the hinge brace.** Disassemble the lid and use the techniques in Step 8 to sand the parts and to glue and screw them together. With a combination square, mark a vertical line on the inner face of each side panel, 15 inches behind the front of the box.

14 **Installing the hinge brace.** Place a 41½-inch 1-by-4 on edge inside the box, with its front edge against the vertical line from Step 13 and its top edges flush with the tops of the side panels. Temporarily secure the board with two corner clamps. Using a combination square, transfer the board's center line to the outside of each side panel, and mark for screw holes 1 inch and 2½ inches from the panel's top. Drill counterbored shank holes and pilot holes at each mark, and fasten the hinge brace with 2-inch No. 10 screws. ▶

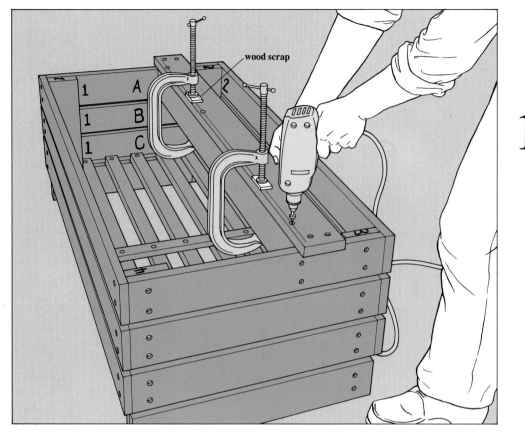

15 **Attaching the hinge rail.** Mark screw-hole positions 1⅛ inches from each end of a 44½-inch board and 1 inch from each edge. Draw a line ⅜ inch from one edge of the board, and mark across it for screw holes 4 inches and 16 inches from each end. Drill counterbored shank holes for 1½-inch No. 10 screws at each mark. Align the board flush with the front of the hinge brace, with its line of edge holes in front, centered on the brace, and its ends overhanging the box by ¾ inch. Temporarily secure the board with C clamps, protecting its face with wood scraps. At each shank hole, drill a pilot hole (*left*). Fasten the rail with the screws.

17 **Marking the lid.** Align the lid with the hinge rail, push it tightly against the open hinge and faintly mark the hinge's ends on the lid. Then pull the lid back a few inches, rotate the open hinge 90° and set it on the lid's top and edge, without turning the hinge end for end. Align the hinge ends with the pencil marks, and mark the lid's edge through screw holes at each end of the hinge and in the middle. Make matching Xs on one end of the hinge and on the lid's adjacent edge, to avoid misalignment later. Drill 3/32-inch pilot holes at each mark on the lid and on the hinge rail for the hinge's screws.

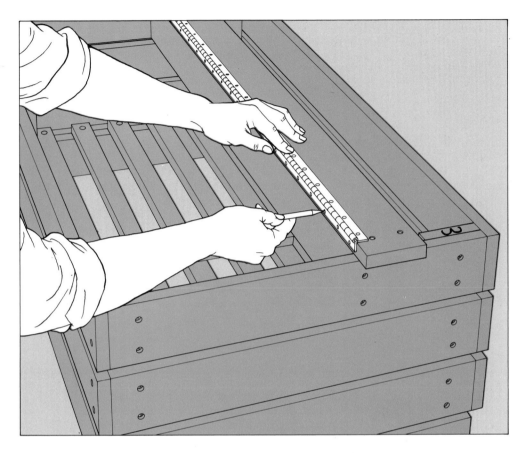

16 **Aligning the hinge.** On a 4-foot length of 1½-inch continuous hinge, make a line with a felt-tip marker 43½ inches from one end. Fold the hinge closed, clamp it to a worktable and use a hacksaw fitted with a carbon-steel blade to cut it. Smooth any sharp edges with a file. Fold the hinge open as far as it will go, then place one leaf flat atop the hinge rail, leaving a ½-inch space at each end. Make a pencil mark on the rail's edge through predrilled holes in the vertical hinge leaf, near each end of the leaf and in the middle. Leave the hinge in place and proceed to Step 17.

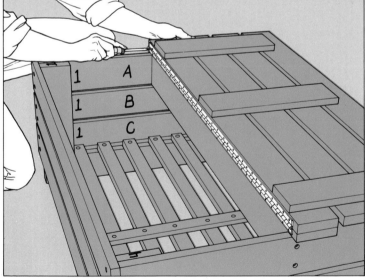

18 **Fastening the hinge.** Open the hinge flat and hold its marked leaf against the lid's rear edge. Drive screws through the hinge leaf into the pilot holes drilled in the preceding step, then drill ³⁄₃₂-inch pilot holes through each additional hinge hole and drive in screws. Rest the lid's top on the hinge rail as if the lid were open, and drive screws through the remaining leaf into the predrilled pilot holes in the rail. Finally, fasten this leaf as you did the other one.

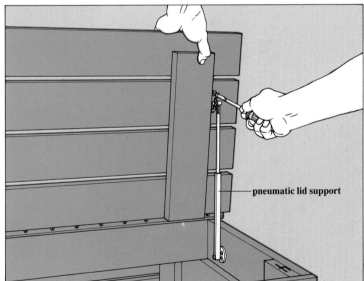

pneumatic lid support

19 **Installing the lid support.** Hold the lid support in its closed position outside the box, placing one end on the box's side panel and the other end underneath the lid to determine the support's eventual position. Hold both ends in place while you open the lid until it is vertical. Adjust the support's position until the lid closes and opens smoothly. Install the support at matching points inside the box: Hold each end in place and mark for pilot holes, then at each end drill one hole and install one screw *(above)*. Test the support again, adjusting its placement if necessary; when it works perfectly, install the remaining screws. Finally, fill all counterbored holes with dowel plugs *(page 51, Step 9)*.

A stylish banquette for seating and storage

For a family room or kitchen where seating and storage are both in demand, the upholstered banquette shown below can fill the two needs simultaneously. Its hollow interior provides nearly 5 cubic feet of storage for seldom-used gear such as canning equipment or Christmas ornaments. The box's lid is a seat; with a backrest it offers comfortable seating for two adults or three children. And the banquette's clean design blends with any room when its upholstery fabric complements the surrounding styles and colors.

All of the banquette's structural components are ¾-inch birch plywood. This versatile material is strong enough to support seated adults, yet light enough to be manageable during assembly and to make the lid readily removable. The smoothness of the birch surface renders the bare interior faces of the box and lid easy to paint. A lumberyard or millwork will cut the various plywood pieces for you. Or, if you have a table saw large enough to accommodate a 4-by-8-foot sheet of plywood, you can do the job at home.

Assembling the box is simple and straightforward, requiring only the basic techniques described on pages 75-77. Trickier and more time-consuming is the job of covering the banquette with foam and fabric. Foam is available at upholstery supply shops, which usually will cut it to your specifications. If you like, you can trim large sheets of foam at home. Use sewing scissors to cut ½-inch foam, a manual or electric carving knife for thicker pieces. On the box's lid and the backrest, the foam will be fastened with spray-on adhesive, then contoured under layers of muslin and cotton batting.

The sturdiest covering for all this padding is a vinyl fabric, such as Naugahyde® fabric, which stretches smoothly and resists stains and tearing. However, vinyl fabrics are available almost exclusively in solid colors. If you prefer patterns, use nylon upholstery fabric with an intricate, nonlinear pattern that does not require matching, and treat the completed banquette with a protective spray, such as Scotchguard® stain repellent. Nylon and vinyl fabrics both can be cut easily with scissors.

Before tacking the fabric to the banquette, practice fastening together scraps of fabric and wood with a tack hammer *(Step 14),* which has a narrow magnetized poll for picking up tacks and a broad poll for driving them home. Bent or misplaced tacks can be pried out with a tack claw *(Step 15).*

Materials List

Plywood	1 sheet A2-quality ¾ ″ birch plywood, 4 ′ x 8 ′, cut into: 1 top piece, 21 ″ x 48 ″; 1 front and 1 back piece, each 10¼ ″ x 46 ″, labeled **A** and **C**; 2 side pieces, each 10¼ ″ x 17½ ″, labeled **B** and **D**; 1 bottom piece, 19 ″ x 46 ″, labeled **E**; 1 base front and 1 base back, each 42 ″ x 3½ ″; 2 base sides, each 14½ ″ x 3½ ″; 1 backrest piece, 9½ ″ x 48 ″	**Cotton batting**	1½ yards cotton batting, ½ ″ thick, cut into 1 lid piece, 27 ″ x 54 ″ 1½ yards cotton batting, 1 ″ thick, cut into 1 back piece, 13 ″ x 54 ″
Lumber	4 strips ¾ ″ quarter-round molding, 8 ″ long, for glue blocks 6 2 x 2 glue blocks, 3 ″ long 3 strips ¾ ″ x ¾ ″, 8 ′ long, cut into: 4 cleats, 44¼ ″ long; 4 cleats, 15¾ ″ long	**Upholstery fabric**	4 yards fabric, 54 ″ wide, cut into: 1 box piece, 17 ″ x 144 ″; 1 lid piece, 33 ″ x 60 ″; 1 back piece, 17 ″ x 60 ″
Polyurethane foam	2 pieces ½ ″-thick standard-density foam, 14 ″ x 68 ″ 1 top piece 3 ″-thick high-density foam, 23 ″ x 50 ″ 1 back piece 2 ″-thick medium-density foam, 11½ ″ x 50 ″	**Hardware**	46 No. 10 flat-head wood screws, 1½ ″ long 32 10/24 T nuts 16 10/24 flat-head machine screws, 1½ ″ long 16 10/24 flat-head machine screws, 1¼ ″ long 12 ring-shanked panel nails, 1 ″ long 60 decorative brass nails, ⅝ ″ long, with heads about ⁷⁄₁₆ ″ in diameter 1 lb. box No. 3 upholstery tacks 3 keyhole hanger plates for No. 10 screws, each with 2 mounting screws 3 No. 10 flat-head wood screws, 2 ″ long
Muslin	2 yards muslin, 48 ″ wide, cut into: 2 lid pieces, 9 ″ x 56 ″; 2 lid pieces, 9 ″ x 27 ″; 1 back piece, 20 ″ x 58 ″	**Adhesives and finishing materials**	wood putty carpenter's wood glue spray foam-and-fabric adhesive 1 quart semigloss latex paint

A storage banquette. Beneath layers of padding and sleek upholstery is a capacious plywood box screwed to a recessed wood base. Wood glue blocks reinforce the corners of box and base from the inside. Padded with polyurethane foam, the box is covered by upholstery fabric that is secured with tacks; the fabric's edges inside the box are hidden by wood cleats. The lid and the plywood backrest are upholstered similarly, but they receive thicker layers of foam, whose edges are rounded by layers of tightly wrapped muslin and cotton batting.

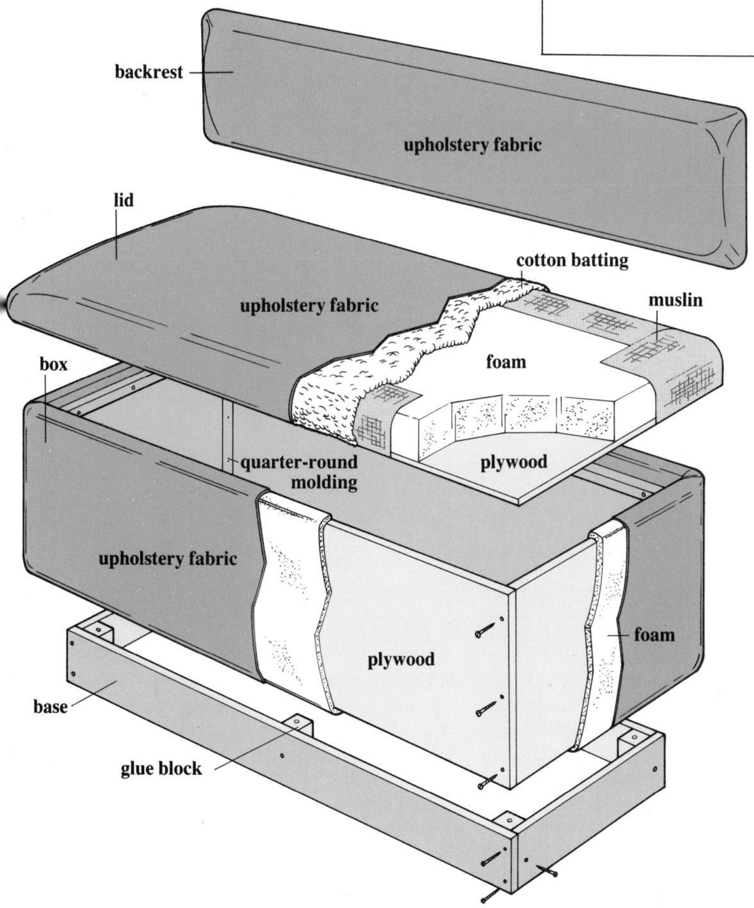

backrest
upholstery fabric
lid
upholstery fabric
cotton batting
muslin
box
foam
quarter-round molding
plywood
upholstery fabric
foam
plywood
base
glue block

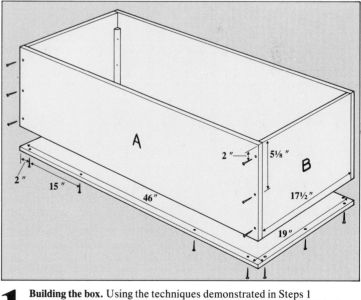

1 **Building the box.** Using the techniques demonstrated in Steps 1 through 6 on pages 76-77, assemble a basic box 46 inches long, 19 inches wide and 11 inches high; attach the bottom to the long sides with screws placed 2 inches and 15 inches from each end. Reinforce each corner of the box with an 8-inch glue block made of ¾-inch quarter-round molding nailed into place with three 1-inch ring-shanked panel nails. Fill all nail and screw holes with wood putty. ▶

2 **Assembling the base.** Stand the base's four 1-by-4s in a rectangle, lapping the long pieces over the short ones. Fasten one corner joint together with two corner clamps; clamp the long piece of the assembled corner flat to a worktable, letting the corner clamps overhang the table edge. Drill two counterbored screw holes for 1½-inch No. 10 flat-head screws through the long 1-by-4 into the short one, 1 inch from the long piece's sides and ⅜ inch from its end. Drill the three remaining corners similarly. Reassemble the rectangle. At each corner, smear glue on the end of the short piece and fasten it to the end of the long piece with screws *(right)*.

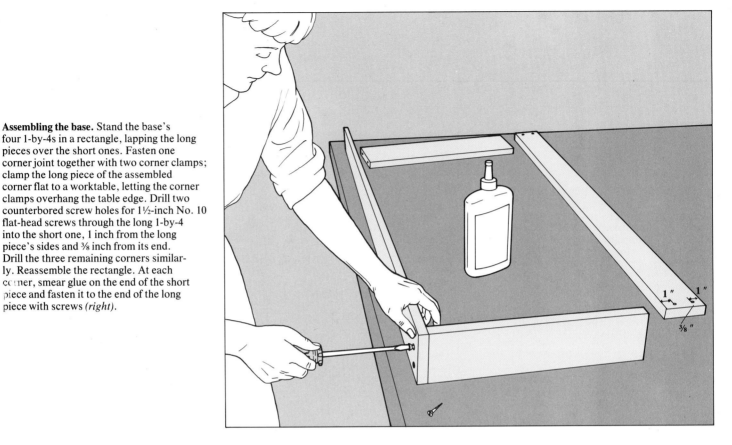

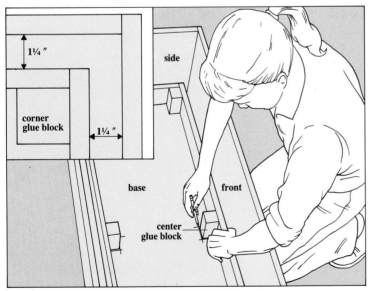

4 **Aligning the base.** Inside the box make marks along the bottom, 1¼ inches from one long panel, which will become the front, and from each side. Set the base in the box, its outer edges aligned with the marks *(inset)*, and trace the outline of each glue block onto the bottom *(above)*. Then place the base on the floor and set the box on top of it, letting the front and sides overhang the base by 2 inches, measured from the outer face of the box to the outer face of the base. At the traced outline of each center glue block, drive a sixpenny nail through the bottom of the box into the block; leave the nailhead protruding for easy removal.

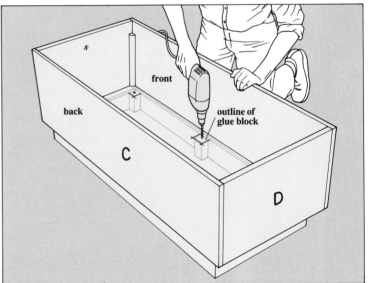

5 **Joining the box and base.** Drill a counterbored hole for a 1½-inch No. 10 screw through the box's bottom into each corner glue block, and drive two screws into the holes at diagonally opposite corners. Remove the protruding nails from the center blocks with a claw hammer, protecting the bottom of the box with a thin wood scrap placed under the hammer's head. Drill a counterbored hole into each center block *(above)*. Turn the box on its side, and mark adjacent Xs on the inner face of one of the base's boards and on the box's bottom; then unscrew the base. Using a sanding block, smooth the base's outer faces with medium and fine (100- and 150-grit) sandpaper, slightly rounding the corners and bottom edges. Refasten the box to the base with all six screws.

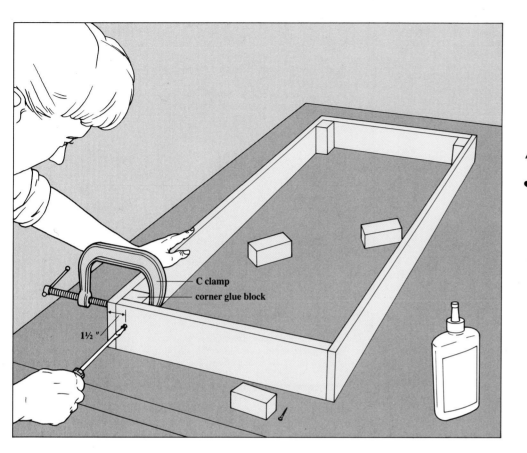

3 **Reinforcing the base.** At each corner of the base, clamp a 3-inch block of 2-by-2 across the long board. Drill a counterbored shank hole for a 1½-inch No. 10 wood screw halfway down the height of the short board and 1½ inches from the corner; drill a matching pilot hole in the block *(page 122)*. Remove the clamp and smear glue on the block, then replace the clamp and fasten the block with a screw driven through the predrilled holes. Install glue blocks similarly at the center of each long board. Cover all the screwheads with putty.

C clamp
corner glue block
1½"

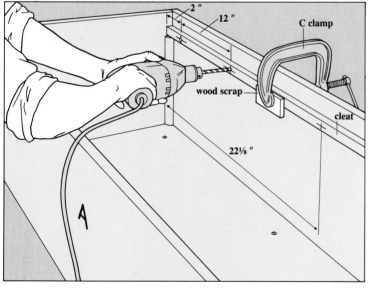

2"
12"
C clamp
wood scrap
cleat
22⅛"
A

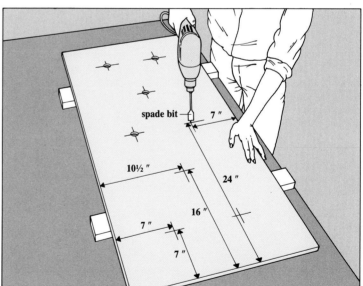

spade bit 7"
10½"
24"
16"
7"
7"

6 **Fitting cleats.** Along the center of a 44¼-inch strip of square ¾-inch stock, make marks for screw holes 2 inches and 12 inches from each end and in the middle. Rest the strip, or cleat, on the quarter-round glue blocks at the box's back, and clamp it. At each mark use a ⅜-inch bit to drill a shallow counterbore; extend the hole through both the cleat and the box with a ¼-inch bit. Unclamp the cleat, and mark matching letters for reference on its back near one end and behind it on the box. Fit another 44¼-inch strip to the box's front similarly.

Draw lines across the side panels between the glue-block tops. Center a 15¾-inch strip atop each line. Clamp, drill and mark each strip as you did the others, placing a hole in the middle and 2 inches from each end.

7 **Drilling air holes.** Mark the lid of the box for two rows of three holes 7 inches from each long side, placing a hole in the middle of each row and 7 inches from each end. Make marks for a third row of holes midway between these two, with holes 16 inches from each end of the lid. Use a ¾-inch spade bit to drill a hole at each mark. To avoid splintering the wood, first drill halfway through the lid, stopping when the bit's point breaks through the opposite face. Turn the lid over and finish each hole from the other side. ▶

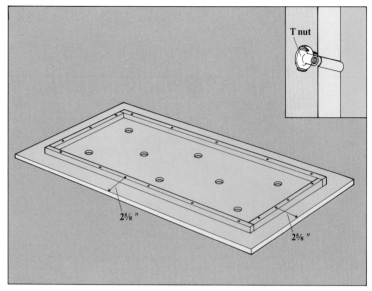

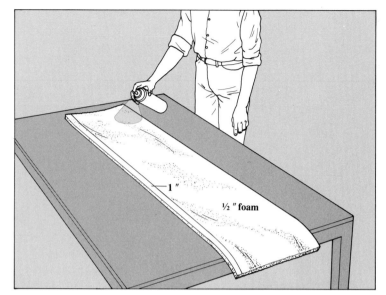

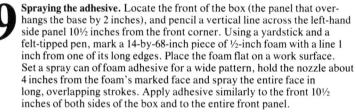

8 **Fitting cleats to the lid.** On the lid's smoother face, which will become its inside face, mark lines 2⅝ inches from each edge. Mark screw holes on two 44¼-inch strips of square ¾-inch stock and on two 15¾-inch strips, using the measurements in Step 6. Clamp, drill and label each strip as you did in Step 6, marking matching letters for reference behind the cleats on the lid. Set the cleats aside and use a hammer to tap a 10/24 T nut *(inset)* into each screw hole on the outside of the box and the lid. Sand the exposed portions of the box's interior, the cleats and the lid's inner face with medium and fine (100- and 150-grit) sandpaper, taking care not to obliterate the marked letters; then paint the sanded surfaces with two coats of semigloss latex paint. Paint the box's base similarly.

9 **Spraying the adhesive.** Locate the front of the box (the panel that overhangs the base by 2 inches), and pencil a vertical line across the left-hand side panel 10½ inches from the front corner. Using a yardstick and a felt-tipped pen, mark a 14-by-68-inch piece of ½-inch foam with a line 1 inch from one of its long edges. Place the foam flat on a work surface. Set a spray can of foam adhesive for a wide pattern, hold the nozzle about 4 inches from the foam's marked face and spray the entire face in long, overlapping strokes. Apply adhesive similarly to the front 10½ inches of both sides of the box and to the entire front panel.

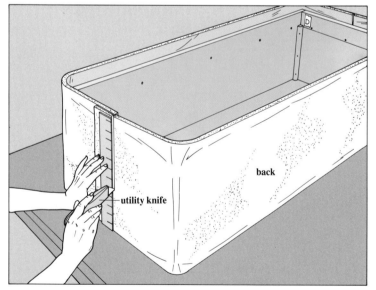

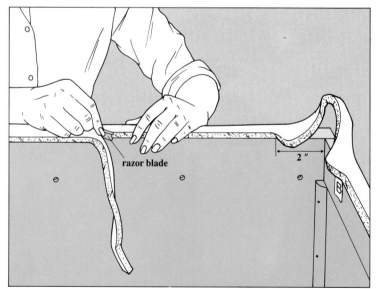

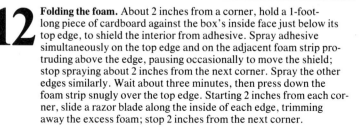

11 **Joining the foam.** Use the techniques of Step 9 to mark the remaining piece of ½-inch foam and to spray it and the remainder of the box with adhesive. Wait two or three minutes, then — on the box's left side — align the new foam's 1-inch line with the box's top, and butt the new piece's end against the first piece. Wrap the new piece snugly around the box and press it down, lapping its end over the first piece. Align a ruler with the underlying piece's end, and cut along the ruler with a utility knife. Peel away the overlapping end, and butt the new piece to the old one.

12 **Folding the foam.** About 2 inches from a corner, hold a 1-foot-long piece of cardboard against the box's inside face just below its top edge, to shield the interior from adhesive. Spray adhesive simultaneously on the top edge and on the adjacent foam strip protruding above the edge, pausing occasionally to move the shield; stop spraying about 2 inches from the next corner. Spray the other edges similarly. Wait about three minutes, then press down the foam strip snugly over the top edge. Starting 2 inches from each corner, slide a razor blade along the inside of each edge, trimming away the excess foam; stop 2 inches from the next corner.

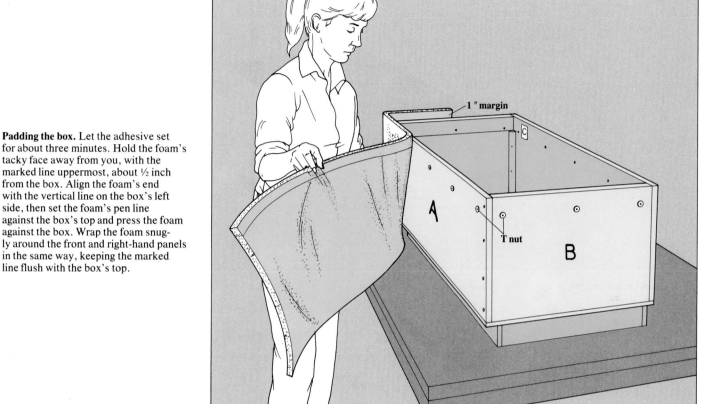

10 **Padding the box.** Let the adhesive set for about three minutes. Hold the foam's tacky face away from you, with the marked line uppermost, about ½ inch from the box. Align the foam's end with the vertical line on the box's left side, then set the foam's pen line against the box's top and press the foam against the box. Wrap the foam snugly around the front and right-hand panels in the same way, keeping the marked line flush with the box's top.

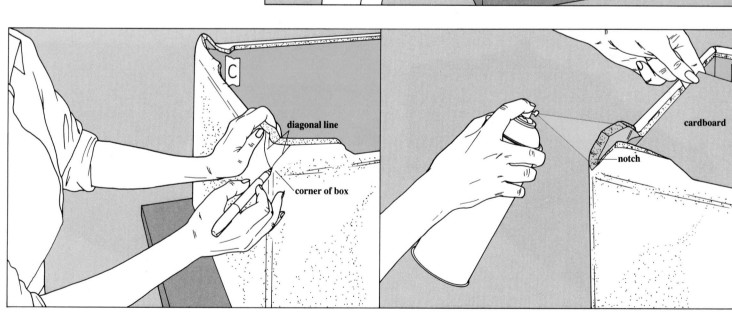

13 **Mitering the foam's corners.** Find the point on the foam directly above one of the box's corners by pressing a finger into the foam. Mark the foam with a felt-tipped pen on each side of the corner, drawing a line up from the corner's point at a 45° angle *(above)*. Cut with scissors along the marked lines, creating a V-shaped notch. Shield the box's interior with the cardboard scrap, and spray adhesive on the inside of the foam and on the edges of the notch and

the box. Fold the foam down on each side of the corner, butting the edges of the V together, then trim away excess foam along the box's inside edge as you did in Step 12. Miter the other corners similarly. Invert the box and fold the foam over its bottom edge *(Step 12)*. Hold a yardstick ¾ inch inside each bottom edge and trim along the yardstick with a razor blade. Miter the bottom corners as you did those at the box's top. ▶

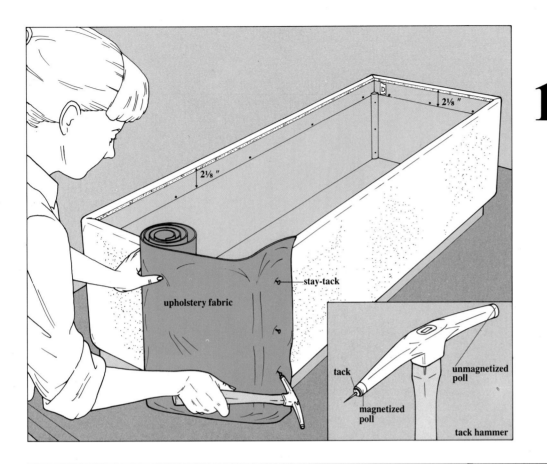

upholstery fabric

stay-tack

tack

magnetized poll

unmagnetized poll

tack hammer

14 **Aligning the fabric.** Draw a horizontal pencil line inside the box 2⅛ inches below its top edge. Cut a piece of upholstery fabric 17 by 144 inches. Hold one end of the fabric vertically 2 inches from the corner on the box's back; fold the fabric's top edge inside the box and align it with the line. While holding the fabric in place, use the magnetized poll of a tack hammer to pick up a single tack by the head *(inset)*. Swing the poll and the magnetically held tack to push the tack lightly through the fabric into the outside of the box's back, about an inch from the fabric's end and the box's top. Then use the hammer's broader, unmagnetized poll to drive the tack halfway home, a process called stay-tacking.

Stay-tack the middle and bottom of the fabric's end to the box's back. Wrap the fabric smoothly around the box, lap it over the three stay-tacks and fasten the end with two more stay-tacks driven in line with the first three.

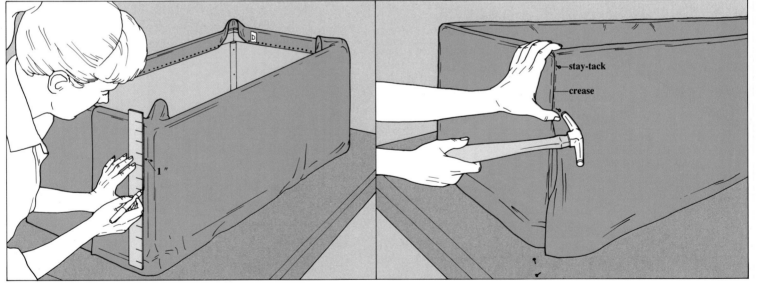

stay-tack

crease

1"

17 **Folding a finished edge.** Pull the overlapping upholstery fabric's end around the corner from the back of the box onto the adjacent side. Using a felt-tipped pen, mark the end's top and bottom 1 inch beyond the corner. Draw a line between the marks *(above)*, and cut the fabric along the line with scissors. Fold 1 inch of the fabric at the end underneath, placing the crease directly over the corner of the box. Finally, drive a column of stay-tacks spaced 3 inches apart just behind the crease *(above, right)*.

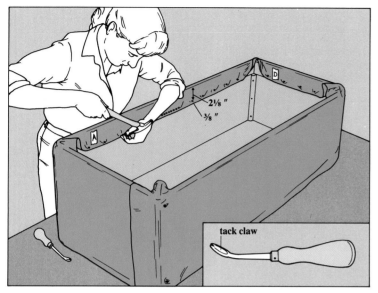

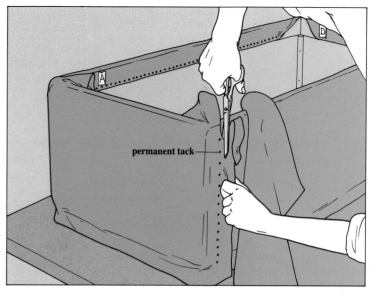

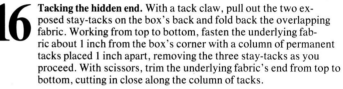
permanent tack

15 **Tacking the fabric's edge.** Inside the box, align the fabric's edge with the marked line. Transfer the cleat letters from the inner sides of the box *(Step 6)* to the fabric that will cover the old letters. Working from the center of one panel toward a corner, drive stay-tacks through the fabric into the box every 4 inches, placing the tacks ⅜ inch from the fabric's edge. Return to the center and stay-tack the panel's other half; then fasten the fabric to the other panels. Working in the same sequence along the edge, slide a tack claw *(inset)* under a stay-tack's head and pry out the tack. As you go, permanently tack the fabric every ½ inch; do not tack the overlapping fabric at the back or within 2 inches of the corners.

16 **Tacking the hidden end.** With a tack claw, pull out the two exposed stay-tacks on the box's back and fold back the overlapping fabric. Working from top to bottom, fasten the underlying fabric about 1 inch from the box's corner with a column of permanent tacks placed 1 inch apart, removing the three stay-tacks as you proceed. With scissors, trim the underlying fabric's end from top to bottom, cutting in close along the column of tacks.

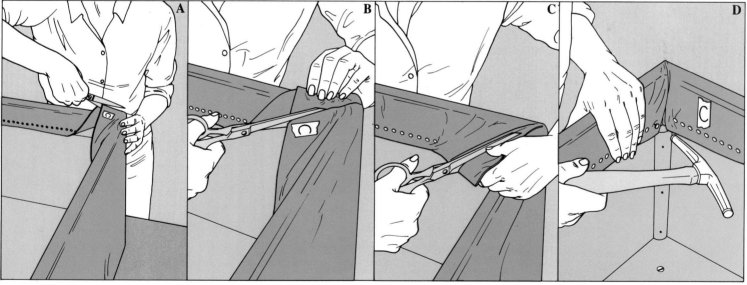

18 **Folding a fabric corner.** With scissors, cut diagonally along the fabric's natural crease to the outside of the box's corner (**A**, *above*). On each resulting flap of fabric draw a line in felt-tipped pen from the scissor cut's tip outward to the fabric's edge, at a 45° angle to the adjacent side of the box. Cut the right flap along the line (**B**), then fold the fabric taut over the box's edge and permanently tack it to the box *(Step 15)*. Cut the left flap parallel to the line but about ½ inch nearer the corner (**C**). Fold the extra ½ inch of fabric underneath the flap, creasing the fabric along the marked line, then fold the flap taut over the box's edge and permanently tack it (**D**). Fold the other three corners similarly. ▶

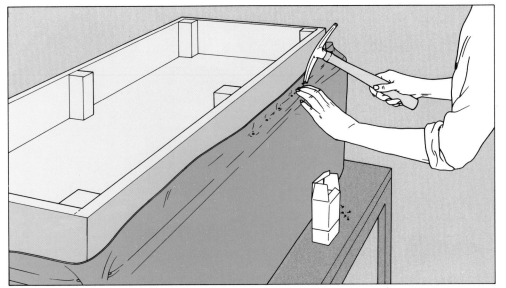

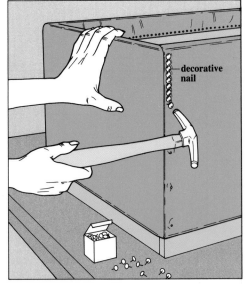

19 **Tacking the bottom.** Invert the box. At each corner pull the fabric snug and secure it with stay-tacks driven into the box's bottom, 2 inches to either side of the corner. Working from the back panel's center toward one corner, pull the fabric up snug and drive in stay-tacks every 4 inches. Secure the fabric on the panel's other half similarly, then on the other panels. Fold the fabric at each corner *(Step 18)*. Removing the temporary tacks as you go, permanently tack the fabric in the sequence used for the stay-tacks, placing permanent tacks ½ inch apart and about ½ inch from the base. Trim the fabric flush with the base, using a utility knife.

20 **Hiding the fabric's end.** Working from top to bottom at the back's left corner, hammer a column of decorative brass nails through the overlapping fabric's folded edge just behind its crease. The nailheads should just touch, forming a solid column of brass hemispheres. As you reach the stay-tacks securing the fabric, remove them with a tack claw. Place another column of decorative nails beside the back's other corner.

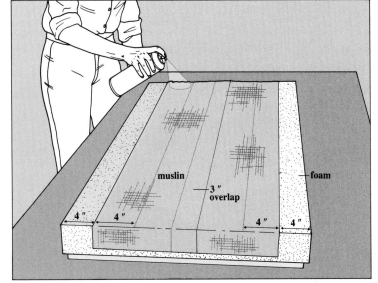

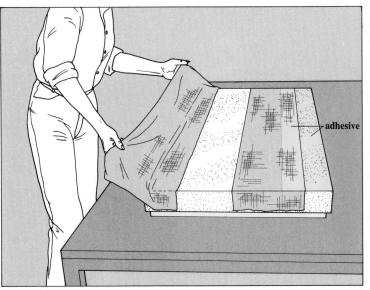

22 **Spraying adhesive on muslin.** Turn the lid foam side up. Cut two 9-by-56-inch pieces of muslin and center them lengthwise on opposite sides of the foam, 4 inches from the long edges. The muslin pieces will overlap in the center of the foam by 3 inches. Spray adhesive on each 4-inch foam margin, then spray the adjacent 4 inches of muslin. Wait three minutes, then proceed to Step 23.

23 **Joining the glued surfaces.** Gently lift the top piece of muslin by its center edge, leaving its glued edge stuck to the adjacent foam. Pivot the muslin outward until the glued 4-inch strips meet, then press the muslin down on the foam. Align the other piece of muslin similarly. Cut two 9-by-27-inch pieces of muslin. Center these pieces across the foam 4 inches from each of its short ends; spray adhesive on adjacent 4-inch strips of muslin and foam, and join the two surfaces. Let the adhesive dry for 10 minutes.

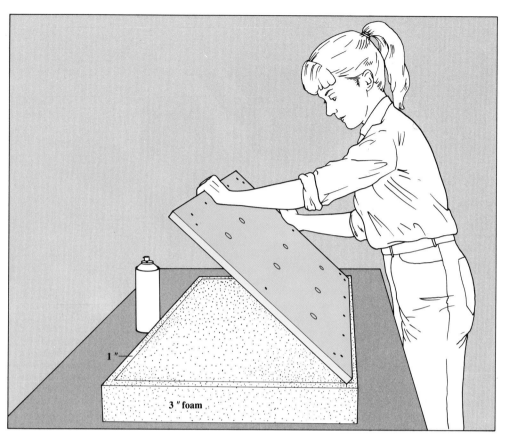

21 **Attaching foam to the lid.** On one face of a 23-by-50-inch piece of 3-inch-thick polyurethane foam, use a yardstick and a felt-tipped pen to mark lines 1 inch from each edge. Spray adhesive on the foam's marked face and on the lid's unpainted face *(Step 9)*. Wait about three minutes, then set one of the lid's long side edges against one of the long lines marked on the foam, and lower the lid onto the foam. Press the lid firmly down, bonding it to the foam.

1 "

3 " foam

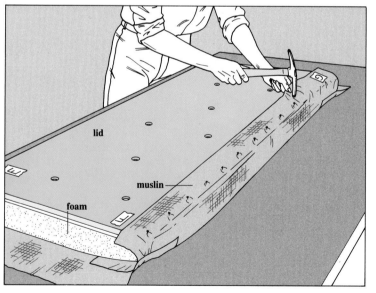

lid

muslin

foam

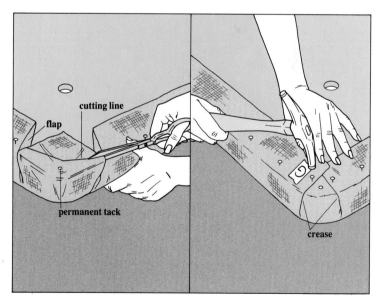

cutting line

flap

permanent tack

crease

24 **Stay-tacking the muslin.** Place the lid foam side down and set the long edges parallel to the worktable's edges. Working from the far edge's center to one corner, wrap the muslin strip around the lid's plywood back, transferring the cleat letter from the wood to the muslin. Pull the muslin toward you and, when it is tight, stay-tack it to the plywood every 4 inches, placing the tacks ½ inch from the lid's edge; do not drive tacks within 2 inches of the corner. Stay-tack the edge's other half in the same way. Then transfer cleat letters, and stay-tack the muslin strips on the other long edge of the lid and on its ends.

25 **Folding a corner.** Pull the pieces of muslin at one corner toward the diagonally opposite corner, creating matching flaps on each side. Place a permanent tack on the diagonal, 1 inch from the corner. On each flap, mark a line ½ inch behind the tack to the point where the crease meets the muslin's edge. With scissors cut away the marked piece of muslin *(above, left)*, trimming just short of the tack. Fold one flap's point inward over the corner's diagonal, placing the flap's crease about ½ inch to one side of the corner; permanently tack the flap. Fold and tack the second flap over the first so that the two creases meet on the plywood in a V that straddles the corner. Fold the other corners similarly. ▶

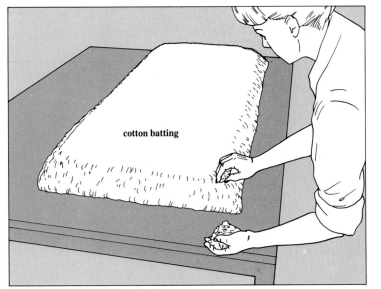

26 Adding cotton batting. Replace the stay-tacks from Step 24 with rows of permanent tacks driven in 1 inch from the lid's plywood edge and placed ½ inch apart. Use scissors to trim the muslin about ½ inch behind the tack line, then draw new pencil lines on the plywood's face 2⅝ inches from each edge. Cut a 27-by-54-inch piece of ½-inch cotton batting. Turn the lid's muslin-covered foam top up and set the batting on the top. Use your fingers to tear away bits of cotton at each corner *(above)*, thinning the batting until the corner is round.

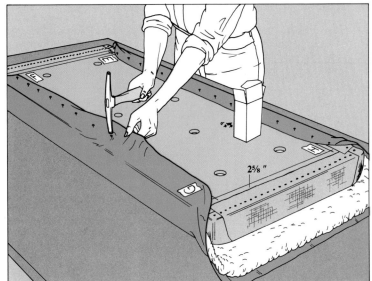

27 Tacking fabric to the lid. Cut a 33-by-60-inch piece of upholstery fabric and place it right side down on the worktable. Center the cotton batting and the lid atop the fabric. On one of the lid's long sides align the fabric with the pencil line, and mark it with the muslin's cleat letter from Step 24. Secure the fabric from the center to each corner with stay-tacks set every 4 inches, placing the tacks ⅜ inch outside the line. On the opposite side pull the fabric snug, then mark and secure it in the same way; mark and stay-tack the ends similarly. Remove each stay-tack and drive in permanent tacks every ½ inch, leaving 2 inches of fabric untacked beside each corner. Fold the fabric's corners *(Step 25)*.

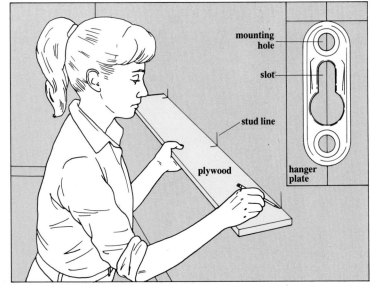

30 Marking the backrest's location. Put the box and lid in position against a wall and, using a carpenter's level, draw a line on the wall 4 inches above the lid. Mark the line's ends by holding the level against the box's sides; move the box away. Just above the line, mark the location of wall studs *(page 124)*. Hold a 9½-by-48-inch piece of ¾-inch plywood against the horizontal line and transfer the stud marks to the plywood. Extend each mark across the plywood with a combination square; mark across each resulting line 3 inches from its starting point. Center a hanger plate on each line, its top against the cross mark *(inset)*. Pencil the slot's outline onto the plywood, and mark the plate's mounting holes.

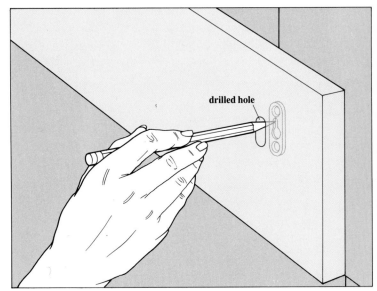

31 Installing hanger plates. From each keyhole outline's rounded bottom to the top of the narrow slot, drill overlapping ⅜-inch holes through the plywood. Pare away any remaining wood by aligning a sharp wood chisel with the edges of the holes and tapping it through the wood with a hammer. Drill ¹⁄₁₆-inch pilot holes at the mounting-hole marks, and screw each hanger plate to the plywood. Set the plywood against the wall's horizontal line with the hanger plates facing the wall, and use a pencil to outline each plate's slot *(above)*. Drill a ⅛-inch pilot hole in the wall at the top of each slot and drive a 2-inch No. 10 flat-head wood screw into the hole, letting the screw's head protrude ¼ inch.

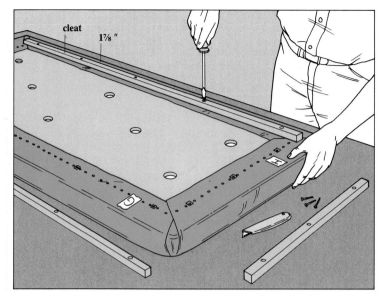

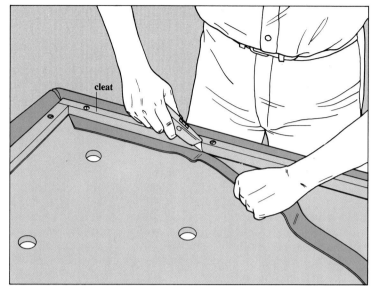

28 **Attaching cleats.** Match the lettered cleats from Step 8 with the letters marked on the fabric. Set one long cleat at a time 1⅞ inches inside the lid's edge, and push an awl through the cleat's holes and the fabric into the holes in the plywood. Enlarge each awl hole by trimming away a ½-inch-square patch of fabric with a utility knife, removing any tacks that interfere. Drive 1½-inch 10/24 slotted flat-head machine screws through the cleat's holes into the lid. Fasten the lid's short cleats similarly, then use the same technique to install cleats inside the box 1⅜ inches below its top, using 1¼-inch 10/24 slotted flat-head machine screws.

29 **Trimming the fabric.** Slide a utility knife along the inside edge of each of the cleats for the lid, cutting away any fabric that extends beyond the cleats. Trim excess fabric below the cleats for the box in a similar fashion.

32 **Upholstering the backrest.** Place the plywood backrest on the worktable with the hanger plates up. Mark trimming lines for the fabric 1½ inches from each edge. Using the techniques in Steps 21 through 27, upholster the plywood's unmarked side: Glue an 11½-by-50-inch piece of 2-inch foam to the wood. Fold a single 20-by-58-inch piece of muslin in half lengthwise and glue it to the foam by halves. Then cover the muslin with a 13-by-54-inch piece of 1-inch cotton batting and a 17-by-60-inch piece of upholstery fabric.

Align the completed backrest's bottom edge with the horizontal line marked on the wall in Step 30, slide the holes in its hanger plates over the protruding screws and lower the backrest onto the screws. If the backrest wobbles, lift it from the wall and slightly tighten the screws.

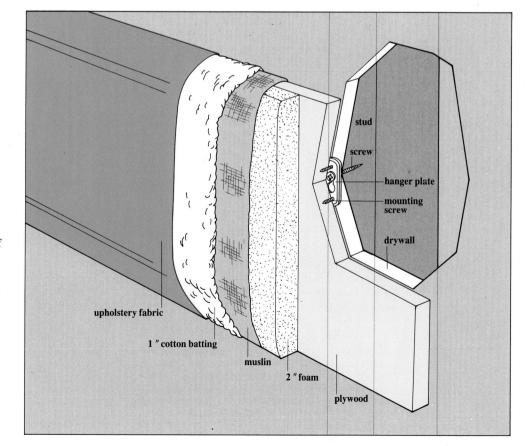

A hand-crafted case for video cassettes

Like books, the cassettes of a video library deserve fitting storage. The sleek plastic case below displays cassettes with panache and practicality: They are stored upright and are separated by dividers to help protect the fragile tapes from dust or distortion. You can build a similar rack for audio cassettes or reel-to-reel tapes by merely adapting and enlarging the design here to suit their dimensions and numbers.

The ideal material for all these cases is ¼-inch acrylic, such as Plexiglas® acrylic, available from plastics suppliers. Unlike wood, the thin acrylic panels can be bonded with nearly invisible joints that do not require either screws or glue. Though slightly more expensive than clear acrylic, colored panels permit greater decorative versatility and mask small mistakes that may be made during assembly.

The factory-finished panels, wrapped in adhesive paper, need careful handling. Leave the protective wrapping intact until assembly but do not rely on it; the plastic sometimes can be scratched through the wrapping. Any minor scratches can be rubbed away with toothpaste, but deep ones call for sandpaper and a buffing wheel *(page 117, Steps 12-13).*

Acrylic demands neat joinery: Mistakes cannot be hidden by putty and paint as in wood. Each piece must be cut precisely with a table saw to ensure smooth, perfectly square edges. Plastics dealers can saw pieces to your needs; if you cut the pieces at home, use a hollow-ground plywood blade with at least six teeth per inch or a carbide-tipped plastics blade. Since the cumulative effect of tiny manu-

facturing variations in the acrylic's thickness may cause the box's overall width to vary, the top and bottom are cut an extra ¼ inch long and the overhanging ends are later sanded flush with the sides. The back is fitted to the assembled box's exact width, either by having it cut or by sanding down a slightly oversized piece.

During assembly, each piece being added is sandwiched between a custom-made spacer block *(box, opposite)* and the upright blade of a combination square, which together hold the piece at right angles to the one it will join.

The two pieces are then fastened together by solvent bonding, a simple method of fusing two plastic pieces. A small, needle-tipped applicator is used to trickle solvent along the joint between the pieces. Drawn into the joint by capillary

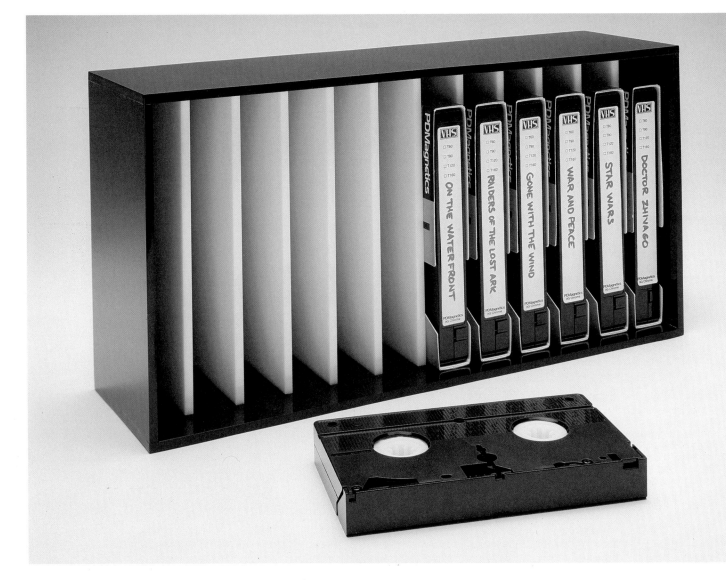

action, the solvent softens the surfaces, then evaporates, leaving the melded acrylic to harden into a permanent bond.

There are simple tricks to bonding: Use a tiny, barely visible bead of solvent *(page 114, Step 3);* you can practice on scraps of acrylic, available from plastics suppliers. Leave freshly bonded joints undisturbed for three minutes. And — if solvent spills — do not wipe it up; let it evaporate, then rub out the resulting blemish with toothpaste.

The final step in making the box is smoothing the exposed edges, using a sanding block, an array of sandpapers from 80- to 400-grit, two flannel buffing wheels for a power drill, and patience. The finished box, polished with a non-abrasive automobile wax if desired, can be fitted with adhesive-backed felt feet (available from plastics suppliers) and set on a tabletop. Or you can drill holes in the box's back, and screw it to a wall. To clean the box, wash it with tepid water. Then buff it with flannel and wipe with a damp rag to remove static charges. Do not use window cleaner, spray-on wax, ammonia, alcohol or paint thinner.

Materials List

Solvent	capillary-flow acrylic bonding solvent
Feet	6 adhesive-backed felt feet

For VHS Cassettes:

Acrylic Plastic	1 piece ¼ "-thick acrylic plastic, 26 " x 38 ", cut into:
	1 top and 1 bottom, 5 " x about 18½ " 11 dividers, 8½ " x 3½ " 2 sides, 8½ " x 5 " 1 back, 8½ " x about 18 "

For Beta Cassettes:

Acrylic Plastic	1 piece ¼ "-thick acrylic plastic, 20 " x 38 ", cut into:
	1 top and 1 bottom, 4⅝ " x about 18½ " 11 dividers, 7¼ " x 3⅛ " 2 sides, 7¼ " x 4⅝ " 1 back, 7¼ " x about 18 "

A video-cassette box. The simple design of this plastic box exposes only the joint lines between the top, sides and bottom. The back fits within these four pieces, its joints hidden at the box's rear, and covers the rear ends of the recessed dividers. Each joint is bonded with solvent, for neat, virtually invisible connections.

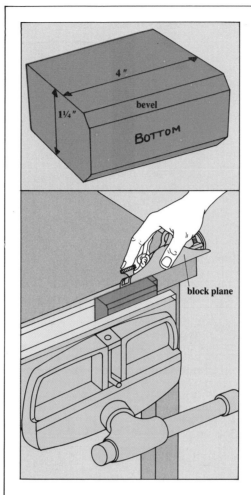

Shaping a Spacing Block

The key to a cassette rack's right-angled joints and evenly spaced dividers is a precisely made wooden spacer block, which is held between dividers during assembly. The block's sides are exactly perpendicular to ensure perfect joints, and its bottom corners are slightly beveled, creating channels for solvent.

The ideal tool for making a spacer is a table saw, either at home or at a mill-work or a plastics supplier. But with care you can do a good job with hand tools and a woodworking vise. Start with a scrap of 2-inch lumber about 6 inches long; shorter pieces are hard to plane. Use a combination square and a knife or an awl to scribe a line exactly 1¼ inches from the block's uncut edge, marking across each end and face. Cut the scrap well to the outside of the line.

Clamp the resulting block in a vise, and use a block plane to shave its cut faces to the line so that the block is precisely 1¼ inches thick. Check each face for squareness; when the block is perfect, label a narrow, unplaned side as the bottom. Hold the plane at a 45° angle to the bottom, and plane a slight bevel (a chamfer) on each adjoining corner. Cut the block to a length of 4 inches.

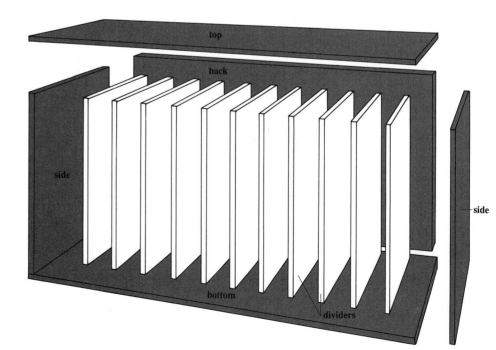

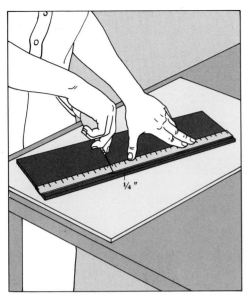

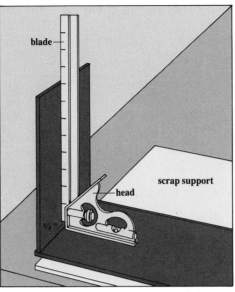

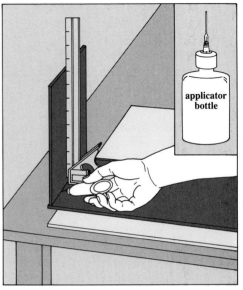

1 **Marking the bottom.** Peel the protective paper off one face of the bottom piece, and set the still-papered face on a clean scrap of acrylic sheet or plywood. Align a long metal ruler ¼ inch from one edge of the acrylic. Hold the point of a scriber or an awl tightly against the ruler, and scratch a line along the entire length of the bottom. Then position the bottom so that its end overlaps the scrap by about ½ inch.

2 **Aligning the first side.** Remove the protective paper from both faces of a side piece, and set the piece upright on the bottom, placing its outer face about ¹⁄₃₂ inch in from the bottom's end to create a tiny ledge for ease in bonding. Slide the end of a combination square's blade about ¼ inch behind the head's perpendicular edge, to make a notch for solvent, then rest the head on the bottom piece and place the blade vertically against the side's inner face.

3 **Bonding the joint.** Invert the solvent applicator (*inset*); with your finger, wipe a drop from its needle. Carefully slide the needle outward from the combination square along the joint's inner edge; maintain a faintly visible solvent line, without dry gaps or a tiny wet trough. Remove the applicator as soon as the solvent reaches the joint's end. Bond the other half of the inner edge similarly and wait three minutes, then bond the joint's outer edge.

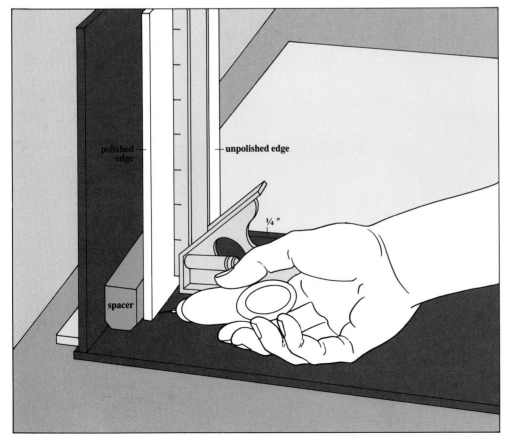

6 **Bonding the dividers.** Set the spacer — its beveled corners down — against the side piece. Remove the paper from a polished divider, and place the divider on end beside the spacer, aligning the unpolished edge with the line scribed on the bottom in Step 1. Rest a combination square's head on the bottom piece, and set the vertical blade snugly against the middle of the divider. Use the technique in Step 3 to bond the joint between the divider and the bottom, working from the square's side. Leave the joint undisturbed for three minutes. Repeat Steps 4 through 6 for the other dividers.

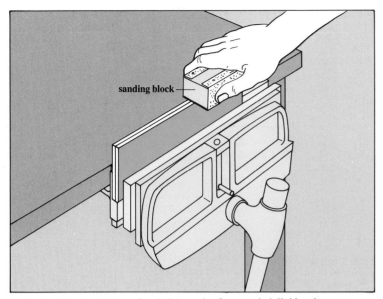

sanding block

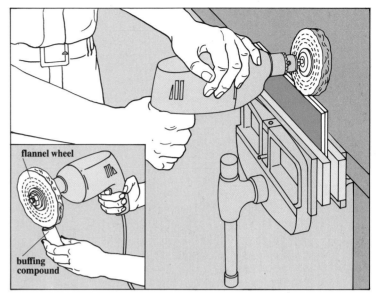

flannel wheel

buffing compound

4 **Sanding the dividers.** Sandwich a pair of paper-clad dividers between scraps of wood; clamp them vertically in a vise, with a long edge horizontal. (Lacking a vise, clamp the sandwiched dividers horizontally to a worktable, with the long edge overhanging the tabletop.) Wrap a quarter sheet of 80-grit sandpaper around a block measuring about 1 by 2 by 4 inches. Sand the long edge, which will be exposed to view in the assembled box, until the saw marks disappear, keeping the block perpendicular to the divider faces. Smooth the edge with progressively finer grits of 100, 120, 150, 220 and 400. Feel the edge with your finger frequently to guard against overheating.

5 **Buffing the dividers.** Fit a power drill with a cotton-flannel buffing wheel. Trigger the drill and lightly hold a stick of buffing compound against the wheel's edge *(inset)* until it gathers a visible coating. Hold the spinning wheel parallel to the dividers for a few seconds, then lightly set it on the edge and traverse repeatedly between the left corner and the center, moving steadily to avoid overheating the plastic. When the buffed half of the edge gleams, reverse the dividers in the vise or clamp. Buff the edge's other half similarly, always avoiding the right corner, which tends to snag the wheel's clockwise rotation. Finally, use a clean flannel wheel without compound to polish each half of the edge.

7 **Adding the second side.** With the bottom's incomplete end overlapping the supporting scrap of ¼-inch plywood or acrylic, set the spacer against the last divider, beveled corners down. Unwrap the second side, and place it on end beside the spacer. Rest the combination square's head on the tabletop, with its vertical blade snugly against the side. Bond the outer edge of the joint between the side and bottom pieces, using the technique in Step 3; after a three-minute pause, remove the spacer, and bond the joint's inner edge. ▶

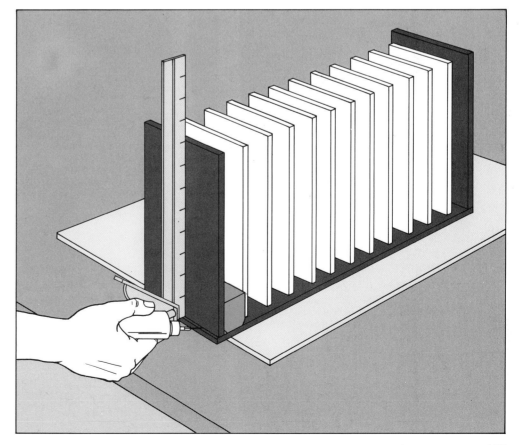

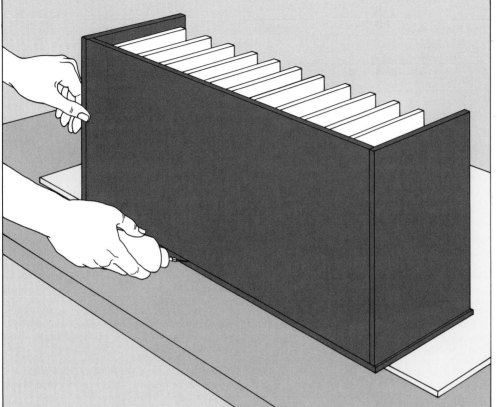

8 **Bonding the back.** With the bottom's rear edge overlapping the supporting scrap, slide the unwrapped back piece between the sides, and press it snugly against the dividers. Bond the length of the joint between the back and bottom, running one long solvent bead from end to end. Immediately press down on the back with one hand while steadily pulling up on the bottom's rear edge with the other hand, to eliminate gaps in the joint. Maintain moderate pressure for about five minutes. Turn the rack on one side; bond the side joint, again applying manual pressure. Secure the other side joint in the same manner.

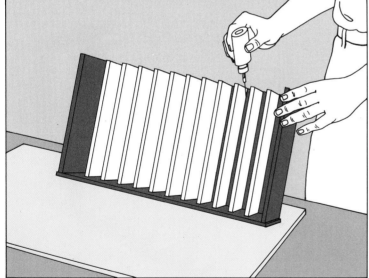

10 **Completing the joints.** Set the rack on its bottom, tilting the unit to put the back at a slight angle from the vertical. On one side of each joint between the dividers and the back, apply a slow trickle of solvent near the joint's top until solvent flowing along the joint reaches the bottom. Bond the inner edges of both joints between the back and the sides in the same way.

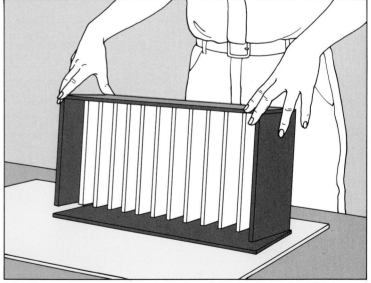

11 **Bonding the top.** Unwrap one face of the top piece and put the piece on the work surface, papered face down. Position the box's open top on the new piece, placing one of the box's sides fractionally behind the piece's end, then aligning the front edge of each side with that of the top piece. Working from outside the box, bond the joint between the back and the top, and press down firmly for about five minutes to eliminate gaps. Bond each side similarly. Turn the box on its back, tilting the top slightly from the vertical, and use the technique in Step 10 to bond each divider to the top. Bond the inner edge of each side joint in the same way.

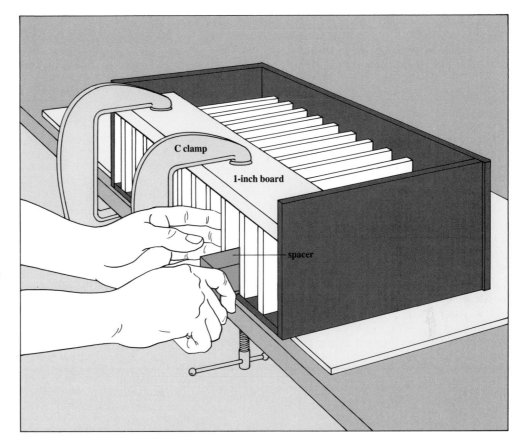

9 **Aligning the dividers.** Set the box on its back with the open top at the table's edge. Place a scrap 1-inch board across the dividers and fasten it loosely with two clamps. Adjust the clamping pressure until it allows a divider to slide fractionally sideways and holds the divider in its new position. Working from right to left, set the spacer on the back in each of the box's openings and gently slide the left divider sideways to the spacer. When all of the dividers are aligned, slightly tighten the clamps. Bond the top 3 inches of the joint between each divider's rear edge and the back, then wait about 90 minutes for the joints to cure.

C clamp

1-inch board

spacer

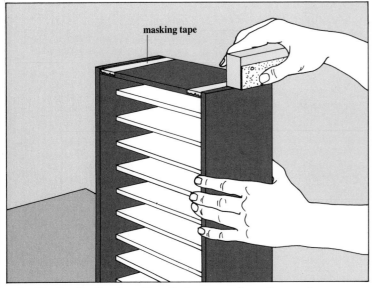

masking tape

12 **Sanding the edges.** Place the box on a soft rag. Remove the protective paper from the box's top and bottom; then apply a strip of masking tape to each end of the side and back pieces, aligning the tape with the edges of the top and bottom pieces. Use the narrow side of a sanding block to sand with 80-grit paper along the exposed edges of each piece — top, bottom and sides — until each edge is smooth and is flush with the neighboring edge or face. Take particular pains with the edges of the top and bottom, which extend fractionally beyond the neighboring faces, but be careful not to scratch through the adjoining masking tape. Sand each edge with successively finer grits of 100, 120, 150, 220 and 400.

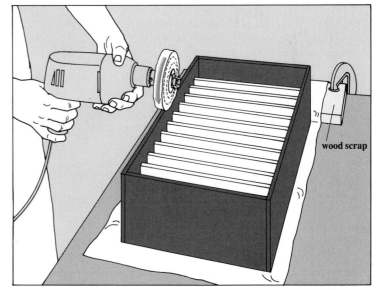

wood scrap

13 **Buffing the edges.** Remove the masking tape from the box. Clamp a wood scrap to the table, and drape rags over the scrap and to its right. Place the box's back on the rags, and set the left side snugly against the scrap. Fit a power drill with a buffing wheel, and charge the wheel with buffing compound *(Step 5, inset)*. Buff the left half of the top and bottom edges, avoiding the right corners. Rotate the box 90°, and buff the left half of the side edges; then rotate the box two more times to buff the other front edges. Buff the exposed edges and ends at the side and back joints in the same way. Use the same sequence to polish the edges with a clean cotton-flannel wheel.

Using power tools safely

Power tools ranging from saber saws to sewing machines are indispensable aids to a home decorator. If purchased wisely and handled properly, the tools on these pages will ensure swift and slick results even for the novice.

In general, inferior tools produce inferior work no matter how experienced the operator may be. When you are looking for shop tools, pass by the least expensive ones. At most hardware stores and home-improvement centers, you should be able to find moderately priced tools of medium to high quality. Look especially for such features as heavy-duty electrical cords, permanently lubricated bearings that simplify tool maintenance, and double-insulated plastic bodies that eliminate the need for a grounded power cord with a three-pronged plug. For projects that call for sewing, you need a sewing machine capable of making straight, zigzag and reverse stitches.

Just as important as buying the right tools is using the right tool for the job. A saber saw, for example, is designed for cutting curves *(below);* although it can make a long, straight cut through plywood, the straight cut will be cleaner and more precise if it is done with a circular saw instead *(opposite).* For tricky angle cuts and maximum precision, a table saw *(pages 120-121)* is best. All power tools come with manufacturer's instructions for care and handling. Take the time to read the instructions, then practice with the tools before you begin a project.

Safety is as important as skill in the operation of power tools, and a few rules apply in every situation:
● Dress for the job. Avoid loose clothing, tuck in your shirt, and roll up your sleeves. Tie back your hair if it is long. And wear goggles when there is a possibility that dust or shavings will fly into your eyes — for example, whenever you are cutting with a circular or table saw or when you are drilling at eye level or overhead. Do not wear gloves when operating power tools; gloves reduce dexterity and can catch in moving parts.
● When operating a power tool, be sure to work on a stable surface; with wood projects, clamp materials to the surface whenever practical.
● Stand comfortably, do not reach any farther than you easily can, and never stand directly in front of — or directly behind — a moving saw blade.

Circular saws tend to kick back toward the operator if the blade gets jammed in the middle of a cut; this generally happens when the sawed section of a workpiece has not been supported as it ought to be to let the saw blade move freely. If the blade should bind while you are making a cut, switch the saw off immediately and support the work to open the cut.

If you are making long cuts in boards or plywood, recruit a helper to support the work for you.
● Always unplug power tools when they are not in use, and whenever you adjust or change parts.

The Saber Saw

Because the blade of a saber saw is only about ¼ inch wide, it can be maneuvered through tight spots and intricate, curved cuts without binding or breaking. With straight cuts, the narrow blade tends to wander from a guideline. But a straightedge guide clamped to the work *(opposite, bottom)* will help keep such cuts on line.

Your best buy is a variable-speed saw that you can speed up along broad curves and slow down for tricky areas. Blades come in sets and individually. Most will cut through wood up to 2 inches thick. Blades with six teeth per inch make fast, rough cuts; blades with 10 to 14 teeth per inch cut more slowly, but also more cleanly. For fine cuts in plywood, buy taper-ground blades with 10 teeth per inch.

To ensure a smooth cut on the good face of a board or panel, work with that surface down. The saber-saw blade cuts on the upstroke, sometimes tearing slivers from the top surface of the work.

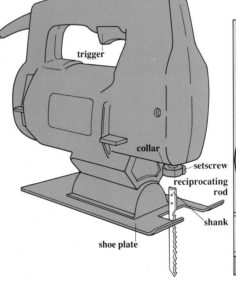

A variable-speed saber saw. A trigger in the handle lets you turn the saw on and off and regulate the speed with which it cuts. To insert a blade, loosen the setscrew in the collar on the reciprocating rod with a screwdriver or a hex wrench, depending on the saw model. Push the notched shank of the blade as far as it will go up into the hollow portion of the reciprocating rod, then retighten the setscrew to anchor the blade.

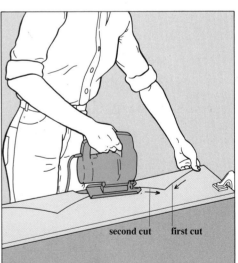

Cutting a curved pattern. Plan cuts so you will not force the blade through an impossibly tight turn; here, both cuts move toward a sharp corner. Rest the tip of the shoe plate on the wood. Start the saw, and guide the blade into the wood, swinging the back of the saw right or left as you move into curves. Do not force the blade, lest it bind or break. If you end a cut with the blade in the wood, let the blade stop before withdrawing it.

The Circular Saw

The easiest way to get wood cut to size is to have it sawed at a lumberyard. To avoid this extra expense, however, you may decide to cut the pieces yourself, using a circular saw *(right)* or table saw *(overleaf)*.

Which saw you use depends on how accurate your cuts must be. The inexpensive, compact and portable circular saw, though designed for rough carpentry, will cut the pieces for many projects with reasonable accuracy. More demanding jobs — such as those calling for close-fitting joints or error-free edges — require a table saw.

The standard circular saw for home use has a 7¼-inch blade that will cut through lumber up to 2 inches thick; for bevels, it tilts to any angle from 45° to 90°. To saw without binding, the motor should develop at least 1½ horsepower.

A variety of blades *(right)* is available for different cutting tasks. Carbide-tipped blades, although more expensive, will outlast ordinary steel blades and save money in the long run.

In operating the saw, a firm grip is extremely important. A 7¼-inch model weighs about 10 pounds and seems heavier at arm's length, when you are cutting large panels. For the added safety of a two-handed grip, buy a saw that has two handles.

A circular saw can be guided freehand for short cuts; for longer cuts, clamp a guide to the workpiece for accuracy *(right)*. The manufactured edge of ¼-inch plywood makes a good, straight guide. Always support lumber from below; without support, the board or panel may crack. Work the saw so that its heavy motor passes over the guide if you are using one.

Many accessories for circular saws are available at hardware stores. A patented metal guide can replace the wood straightedge shown at right. Another guide simplifies rip cutting *(page 39)*. A circular-saw table, which holds a circular saw underneath it upside down, offers a few advantages of the professional's tool — stability and accuracy — at a lower price, but with some loss of versatility.

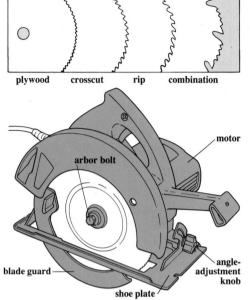

plywood   crosscut   rip   combination

A circular saw. Driven by a powerful motor, the blade of a circular saw cuts on the upstroke. A spring-activated guard, which slides up into the housing of the saw during operation, drops back down over the blade as the cut is finished. The angle-adjustment knob lets the shoe plate be tilted for beveled cuts. The arbor bolt, which holds the blade in place, unscrews so that the blade can be changed.

Blade styles. A fine-toothed plywood blade slices through plywood without splintering it. A crosscut blade's small teeth tear smoothly across the grain; a ripping blade's larger teeth, set at a sharper angle, saw with the grain. A combination blade both rips and crosscuts, with small teeth separated by deep indentations.

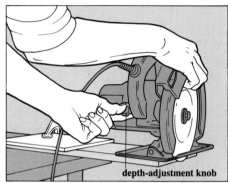

Adjusting blade depth. Loosen the depth-adjustment knob on the back of the saw. Lay the shoe plate flat on the wood and push up the blade guard. With one hand, hold up the guard while grasping the blade housing to support the saw body. Keeping the shoe plate flat, raise or lower the saw body — and with it the blade — until the blade is about ¼ inch below the bottom surface of the board to be cut. Retighten the depth-adjustment knob.

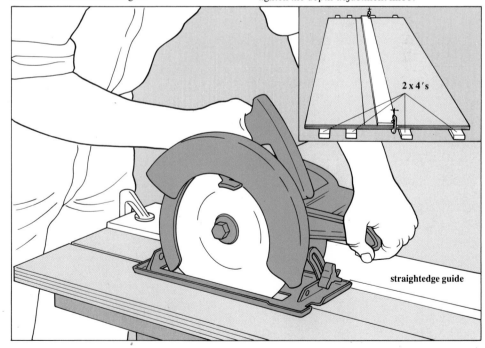

Sawing with a straightedge. Clamp a straightedge to the board to be cut so the blade falls on the waste side of the cutting line. Put on goggles before sawing. To cut a large panel of plywood *(inset)*, rest the panel on the floor, on 2-by-4s. Holding the saw firmly, cut slowly along the straightedge. Do not force the blade — it may bind. Keep a steady grip on the saw as it clears the board, and prepare to catch its unsupported weight.

The Table Saw

The table saw is the versatile tool professional cabinetmakers use for cutting boards with furniture-quality precision. It is the blade's stability and the guides built into the saw's generous work surface that make this accuracy possible.

The saw's fence, an adjustable metal straightedge that slides over the table parallel to the blade, ensures straight cuts as boards are pushed along it into the blade. For angled cuts, the fence-like front face of a calibrated miter gauge guides boards at any angle set on its dial. A blade-tilting mechanism under the table swivels the blade itself, angling it to the wood to make beveled cuts possible. Used in tandem, the miter-gauge dial and blade-tilting crank make it easy to set up tricky compound-angle cuts, which otherwise would be virtually impossible to do accurately.

Bench-top table saws are as precise as full-sized floor models for cutting small pieces of wood. However, large panels of plywood need the greater table area and stability of a standard table saw.

Like circular saws, table saws are sized by the diameter of the blades they use — ranging from 8 to 12 inches. A typical home saw, with a 10-inch blade, can cut 3¼ inches deep. The same types of blades used for a circular saw *(page 119)* are available for a table saw, with larger diameters and center holes. As with circular-saw blades, carbide-tipped table-saw blades last longer than those made of steel.

For cutting small pieces safely, the miter gauge or a push stick should always be used to feed the wood, to keep hands away from the blade. Never stand directly behind the blade: Wood binding in the blade can be kicked sharply backward. Always make sure the saw is disconnected from an electrical outlet and turned off before adjusting the blade.

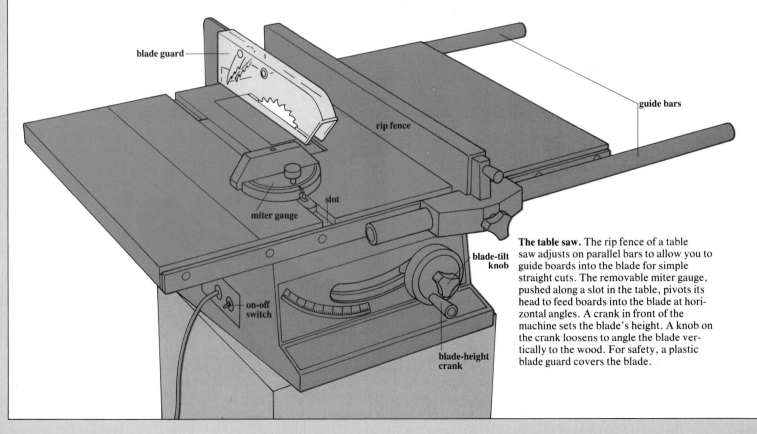

The table saw. The rip fence of a table saw adjusts on parallel bars to allow you to guide boards into the blade for simple straight cuts. The removable miter gauge, pushed along a slot in the table, pivots its head to feed boards into the blade at horizontal angles. A crank in front of the machine sets the blade's height. A knob on the crank loosens to angle the blade vertically to the wood. For safety, a plastic blade guard covers the blade.

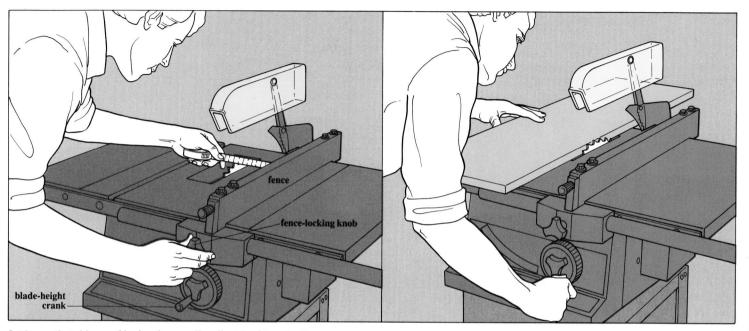

Setting up the table saw. Unplug the saw. To adjust the fence for the width of the cut, loosen the fence's locking knob and measure from the fence to the blade with a ruler or tape measure *(above)*. Position the fence so that the saw kerf — the cut made by the blade — falls just on the waste side of the cutting line. Lock the fence. Turning the blade-height crank *(above, right)*, raise the blade so that its teeth are just slightly higher — no more than ¼ inch — than the piece of wood to be cut.

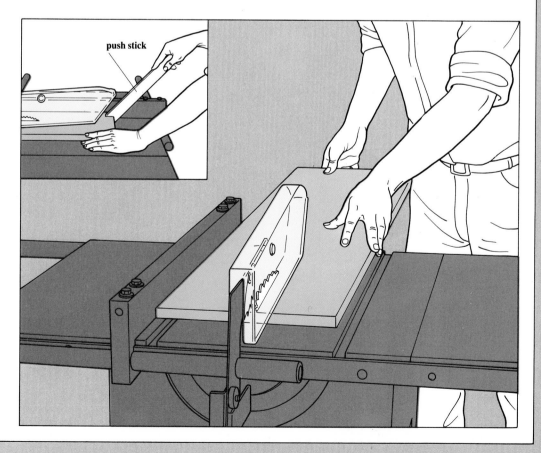

Making the cut. Put on goggles before beginning the cut. Plug in the saw and lower the blade guard. For a large board or panel, station a partner on the opposite side of the saw to support the wood as it passes over the table. Turn on the saw and press the board against the fence, then forward into the blade. When the end of the board nears the blade, advance the wood with a notched push stick *(inset)*, made by cutting a corner out of a scrap of 1-by-2 or 1-by-3.

The Variable-Speed Drill

Like the saber saw, the variable-speed drill works at a variety of speeds, depending on how hard you squeeze its trigger. Small holes in wood are bored at the fastest speeds; slower speeds are better for drilling large holes in wood and for any hole in metal or masonry.

The ⅜-inch drill at right can accommodate bit shanks from 1⁄64 inch to ⅜ inch in diameter. Within that range, many different bits are available to drill holes from 1⁄64 inch to 1½ inches in diameter in wood, metal or masonry. Power drills also can hold the shanks of such accessories as buffing wheels, grinding wheels and hole saws *(page 33).*

In this volume, the drill is most often used to drill the hole for a wood screw that fastens together two boards. This task actually requires three holes: one in the bottom board to grip the screw's threads tightly, and two successively wider holes in the top board for the shank and head. You can use a separate twist bit for each hole, then broaden the top hole with a countersink bit. More simply, you can bore all three holes at once with a counterbore bit, which matches the shape of the screw's threads and shank, and has an adjustable head that bores, or counterbores, a

recess for the screwhead. Avoid cheap counterbore bits: They tend to clog.

Spade bits bore holes up to 1½ inches in diameter; because these bits tend to wobble, use of a drill guide is advisable. The model at right, below, will fit any drill with a threaded shaft.

Masonry bits, with closely spaced, carbide-tipped edges, grind slowly through brick and concrete, which would crumble around a twist bit.

Masonry and spade bits are most often sold singly; countersinks are sold in only one size. Counterbore and twist bits are sold singly and in sets that include the most frequently used sizes.

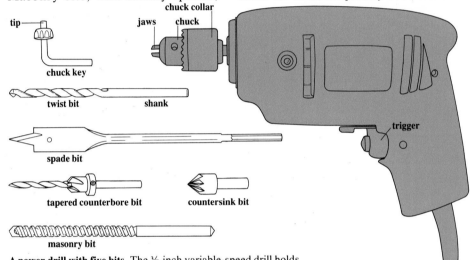

A power drill with five bits. The ⅜-inch variable-speed drill holds twist, spade, counterbore, countersink and masonry bits with shanks up to ⅜ inch in diameter. To insert a bit, turn the chuck collar to open the jaws, push the bit shank between the jaws and tighten the collar by hand until the jaws grip the shank. Then push the tip of the chuck key into one of the three holes in the chuck, and twist the key handle. To change bits, loosen the collar with the chuck key before turning it by hand.

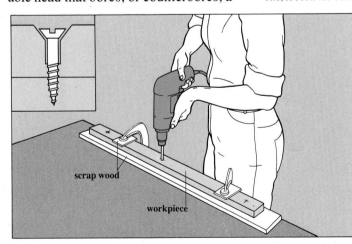

Using a power drill. Clamp the work to a table and indent the wood at the starting point with an awl. To govern a hole's depth, wrap tape around the bit at the required distance from the tip. Set the bit in the dent, squeeze the trigger and push the drill straight down with steady, moderate pressure. To drill holes for a wood screw *(inset)*, use a tapered counterbore bit *(above).* Or drill two holes of increasing size, a narrow one in the bottom piece for the screw's threads and a wide one in the top for the shank. Widen the hole's mouth with a countersink bit if it will be puttied, or use a third twist bit if it will be plugged with a short dowel.

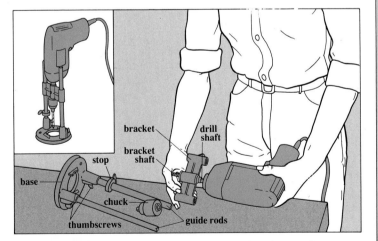

Attaching a drill guide. Remove the drill's chuck. (Most unscrew from the shaft of the drill, but check the manufacturer's instructions.) Twist the guide bracket onto the drill shaft; screw the chuck onto the bracket's shaft. Slip the guide rods through their holes in the bracket, loosen the thumbscrews on the base, set the ends of the rods flush with the bottom of the base, and tighten the screws; this procedure ensures that the holes drilled are perpendicular to the work surface when the drill guide is upright *(inset).* If you want to drill to a certain depth, position the stop on the guide rod after you have inserted a bit in the chuck.

The Sewing Machine

One of the most ingenious home tools, the sewing machine is also one of the easiest to use and maintain. A good machine is virtually trouble-free mechanically and needs only a light oiling every three or four operating hours.

Threading the machine properly is essential; the owner's manual will tell you how. Although every model threads somewhat differently, there are always two threads, an upper thread from the spool and a lower thread wound around the bobbin *(right)*. The tension on the upper thread is adjusted with a knob.

Synthetic thread must be used with synthetic fabric, and natural with natural, so that, in cleaning, the fabric and thread shrink at the same rate. Size 50 thread and a size 14 needle are best for most fabrics, though heavier thread and a size 16 needle make stronger seams in thick fabric, such as canvas.

The number of stitches per inch also affects seam strength. The standard number is 12 to 15 stitches per inch, more if very strong seams are needed.

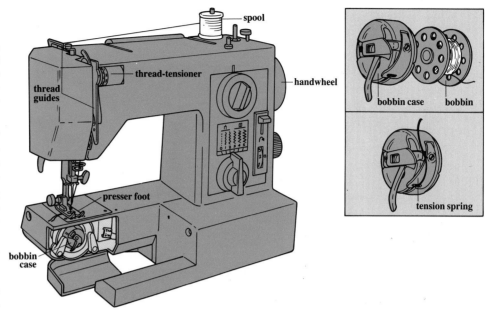

The versatile sewing machine. Every sewing machine has a set of thread guides that take the thread from the spool, through an adjustable thread-tensioner and down to the needle. A second thread is wound around a lower spool called the bobbin *(top inset)* and slipped underneath a tension spring *(bottom inset)* on the bobbin case.

Dials on the machine set the type, length and direction of a stitch. The presser foot, a ski-shaped clamp that holds the fabric flat, comes in a variety of configurations for special stitches. The feed dog, a toothed plate below the presser foot, advances the fabric automatically. The handwheel turns the mechanism to start the first stitch.

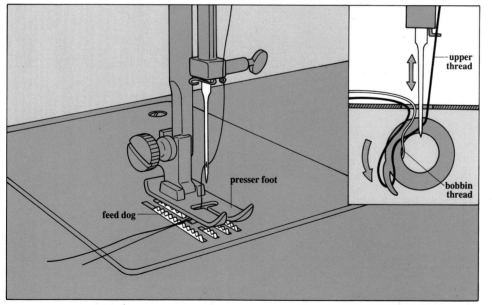

Preparing to sew. After threading the machine, lower the presser foot, grasp the end of the upper thread and turn the handwheel to make the first stitch. As you do this, the upper thread will tighten around the bobbin thread *(inset)* and pull it up in a loop. Raise the presser foot and pull out the end of the bobbin thread from the loop. Draw out both threads 3 or 4 inches and pull the ends together to the rear of the presser foot.

Sewing the fabric. Position the fabric under the needle. Lower the presser foot, turn on the machine, and guide the fabric as the feed dog pulls it forward. When you finish sewing, set the machine in reverse and backstitch over the last few stitches for reinforcement. Then raise the presser foot, pull out the fabric and cut both threads.

The Basic Fasteners

Finding the structural parts of your home is the first step in attaching storage projects securely to the walls or ceiling. Behind the plaster or wallboard skin of the typical wood-frame house is a skeleton of vertical 2-by-4 studs and horizontal 2-by-10 joists. These framing members provide the ideal support for heavy loads.

The most reliable method of finding the framing members in your house is to drill small holes into the wall or ceiling and probe with a wire *(below)*. You can easily fill these holes later with putty or spackling compound.

If the studs or joists are conveniently located, nails or wood screws are the fasteners of choice. Where framing members are unavailable, light loads may be

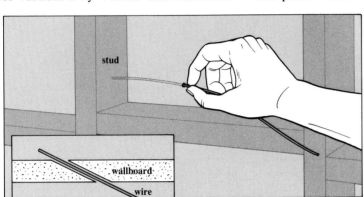

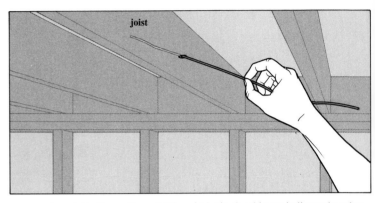

Finding a framing member. With your knuckles, tap lightly across the wall; a solid sound should reveal the approximate position of a wooden stud. To locate a stud precisely, drill a small hole a few inches away from and angled sharply *(inset)* toward the suspected location. Insert a thin, stiff wire until its tip meets the stud. (If you encounter cushiony resistance, the wire is probably running into insulation; try to push the tip on through.)

Grasp the wire at the hole with thumb and forefinger *(above, left)* to mark the distance from hole to timber. Then extract the wire, and position it at the same angle outside the wallboard. The wire's tip should now indicate the edge of the concealed stud; add ¾ inch to find the stud's center. Confirm the location by driving a nail through the wallboard until you feel it enter the wood.

Use the same process to locate a joist *(above, right)*. When drilling overhead, wear safety goggles to keep plaster dust out of your eyes.

To determine a point anywhere else along the center line of any framing member you have located, measure an equivalent distance from an adjacent wall, then confirm by driving a nail.

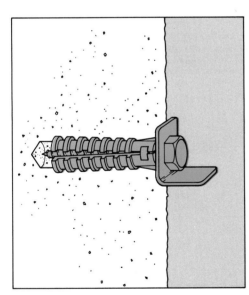

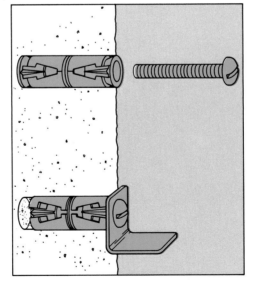

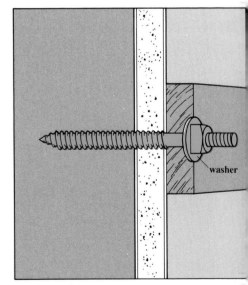

Lag bolt. Sometimes called a lag screw, this big fastener holds a very heavy load. To use it in a stud, drill a pilot hole slightly smaller in diameter than the bolt. Slip the bolt through the hanger of the object to be hung, then drive it into the hole by turning its head with a wrench. In masonry *(shown)*, drill a hole deep enough for the bolt and wide enough so a matching-sized lag shield fits tightly; the flanges at the outer end of the shield should bite into the masonry. Tap the shield into the hole before driving the bolt into the shield.

Expansion shield. This metal device with interior threads is used with a matching machine screw to hold a load on masonry or a thick plaster wall. Drill a hole that will hold the shield snugly, and tap the shield into it. Make sure the screw is long enough to extend through the hanger of the object being hung and the length of the shield. As you tighten the screw, wedges in the shield will be pulled toward the middle, pushing the cylinder sides hard against the masonry or plaster.

Hanger bolt. The advantage of this heavy-duty fastener is that you can fix it in the wall before the load is hung on it. One end is threaded like a wood screw, the other machine-threaded to take a nut. Drill a pilot hole slightly smaller than the bolt diameter into a stud. Drive the bolt in by turning it with locking-grip pliers grasping the middle section. Slip the hanging object over the protruding end and fasten it with a nut. If the hanging object is wood, as here, use a washer so the nut will not gouge the wood surface.

attached with expanding anchors that grip the edges of holes drilled into the wallboard or plaster. For heavier loads you need toggle bolts or Molly® bolts, which cling to a wall or ceiling by squeezing from both sides *(bottom)*.

Other expanding anchors are available for masonry walls, which can bear a load at any point. If the surface of a masonry wall is exposed and you have a choice, the mortar joints are a better place to drill than the brick or block, since mortar is comparatively soft and easy to patch.

In recent years the partition walls of many apartment buildings have been built with metal studs. Self-tapping screws, with sharp threads that hold tightly in sheet metal, are recommended for this type of construction.

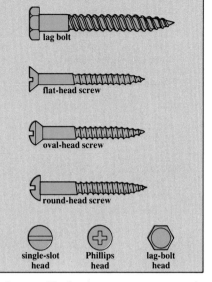

Wood screws. Flat-head screws are countersunk flush with the surface or hidden beneath plugs or putty. Round and oval heads can be left exposed. Heads have one slot or, for a Phillips screwdriver, two crossed slots. Phillips heads are less likely to rip under turning pressure. Screw-shaft diameters are denoted by gauge numbers: The higher the number, the larger the diameter. Diameters of lag bolts, whose hexagonal *(shown)* or square heads are turned by wrenches, are expressed in inches (from ¼ to 1 inch).

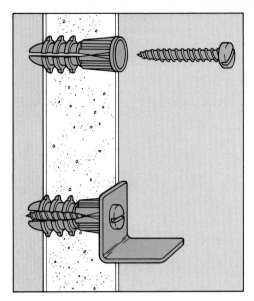

Anchor. The sides of an anchor press out to gain a tight grip in masonry, wallboard or plaster when a matching-sized screw is driven into it. A plastic anchor *(above)*, sufficient for light loads, can be used with a wood screw or a self-tapping screw *(shown)*. Heavier weights need lead anchors. With either type, first tap the anchor into a hole drilled to fit it snugly. (In wallboard, as here, the anchor and screw should be long enough to extend through it.) Then insert the screw through the object to be hung, and drive it into the anchor.

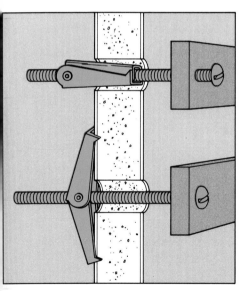

Toggle bolt. A toggle bolt must be long enough for its wings to spring open and grip the inside of a hollow wall. Drill a hole large enough for the folded wings to pass through, but do not push them in at this stage. Unscrew the wings from the bolt, slip the bolt through the object to be hung, and replace the wings. Then push the bolt through the wall; when the wings pop open, the bolt will feel loose in the hole. Pull the device back so that the wings will bite into the inside of the wall as you tighten the bolt.

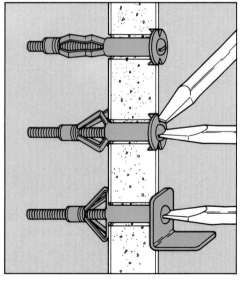

Molly bolt. The unbroken cylinder near the bolthead of one of these hollow-wall anchors should be as long as the wall is thick. Tap the Molly into a hole drilled to its diameter. Wedge a screwdriver into one of the indentations in the flange to keep the sheath from turning as you tighten the bolt with another screwdriver. The sheath arms will splay out against the inside of the wall. Do not overtighten, or you may break the Molly's arms. Remove the bolt to put the load on it, then screw it back into position.

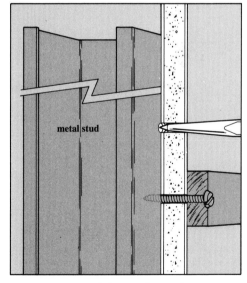

Self-tapping screw. This sort of screw is used to attach weights to metal studs. Drill a small hole in the wallboard to the face of the stud. Make a starter dent in the stud with a center punch and a hammer. Then use a twist bit to drill a pilot hole half the diameter of the screw through the thin metal. Insert the screw through the object you are hanging, and drive it into the stud; the screw should be long enough to reach about ½ inch beyond the face of the stud.

Acknowledgments

The index for this book was prepared by Linda Busetti. The editors are particularly indebted to Eunice Hearn, Grainline Studio of Sewing, Ellicott City, Maryland. For their help in the preparation of this volume, the editors also wish to thank: Steven Aldrich, Grants Pass, Oregon; Ward Anderson, Osage Products Company, Eldon, Missouri; R. Winston Bell, George C. Brown & Company, Inc., Greensboro, North Carolina; David A. Bennett, Alexandria, Virginia; Logan Bentley, Rome; Gerry Brack, McLean, Virginia; Caterino Chiara, MAP Arredamenti, Treviso, Italy; Elizabeth Clarke-Shaw, Creative Pastimes, Columbia, Maryland; Jim Cooper, New York; Carolyn Fleig, Santa Fe, New Mexico; Dr. and Mrs. Sam Harrington, Washington, D.C.; Horst Huttner, Blair, Inc., Baileys Crossroads, Virginia; Renate Littmann, Schöner Wohnen, Hamburg; Veronica McNiff, New York; Paul J. Mathis, Alexandria, Virginia; Gabriella Reali, Mondadori, Milan; Regina Rector, Cornell University, Ithaca, New York; Christine Schuyler, Washington, D.C.; Barbara Schwartz, Dexter Design, New York; Jerry Siegel, W. S. Jenks & Son, Washington, D.C.; Scot Terrell, Alexandria, Virginia; Carl W. Townsend, Nelson Beck of Washington, Inc., Washington, D.C.; Chris Unks, Case Design/Remodeling, Washington, D.C.; Nelson H. Wurz, Nelson Beck of Washington, Inc., Washington, D.C.; Charlotte Young, Iowa State University, Cedar Rapids, Iowa.

Picture Credits

The sources for the photographs in this book are listed below, followed by the sources for the sketches. Credits from left to right on a single page or two-page spread are separated by semicolons; credits from top to bottom are separated by dashes.

Photographs: **Cover:** Larry Sherer, photographer / clothes, courtesy Inge's, Alexandria, Virginia / shoes, courtesy Bradshaw's Shoes, Alexandria, Virginia. **2, 3:** MAP Arredamenti S.p.A., Treviso, Italy. **4:** Robert Lautman, photographer. **5:** Nörenburg, photographer, published by Gruner Und Jahr, Hamburg. **6, 7:** Robert Perron, photographer / Tim Button, Stedila Design, Inc., New York, designer. **18:** Dan Cunningham, photographer. **22:** Larry Sherer, photographer / key ring and walking stick, courtesy The Pineapple, Inc., Alexandria, Virginia / umbrella, courtesy Placewares, Alexandria, Virginia / leash, courtesy Olde Towne School for Dogs, Alexandria, Virginia. **26:** Dan Cunningham, photographer / shoes, courtesy Bradshaw's Shoes, Alexandria, Virginia, and J. C. Penney, Alexandria, Virginia. **28:** Larry Sherer, photographer / shoes, courtesy Bradshaw's Shoes, Alexandria, Virginia / clothes, courtesy The Talbots, Alexandria, Virginia. **34:** Dan Cunningham, photographer / slippers, courtesy New Zealand Imports, Ltd., Alexandria, Virginia / sweaters, courtesy Smith's of Bermuda, Alexandria, Virginia. **42:** Gordon Kurzweil, photographer / location, courtesy St. Mary's Catholic Church, Alexandria, Virginia / tools, courtesy W. S. Jenks and Son, Washington, D.C. **43:** Larry Sherer, photographer / tools, courtesy Johnson's Flower Center, Washington, D.C. **44:** Larry Sherer, photographer / location, courtesy St. Mary's Catholic Church, Alexandria, Virginia — Gordon Kurzweil, photographer / location, courtesy St. Mary's Catholic Church, Alexandria, Virginia / bicycle, courtesy Tow Path Cycle, Inc., Alexandria, Virginia. **45:** Gordon Kurzweil, photographer / location, courtesy St. Mary's Catholic Church, Alexandria, Virginia / tools, courtesy Strosnider's Hardware, Inc., Bethesda, Maryland. **46:** Gordon Kurzweil, photographer. **48:** Gordon Kurzweil, photographer / F. L. Wall, Arlington, Virginia, designer. **52:** Dan Cunningham, photographer. **56:** Larry Sherer, photographer. **62:** Dan Cunningham, photographer. **74, 78:** John Neubauer, photographer. **84:** Larry Sherer, photographer / location, courtesy Susan and Lloyd Feller / vacuum cleaner, courtesy Appliance Service Center, Alexandria, Virginia. **92:** John Neubauer, photographer / ski equipment, courtesy The Old Town Ski Shop and Outdoor Store, Alexandria, Virginia. **100:** Gordon Kurzweil, photographer. **112:** Dan Cunningham, photographer.

Illustrations: **13-17:** Sketches by George Bell, inked by Frederic F. Bigio from B-C Graphics. **18-21:** Sketches by Roger Essley, inked by Frederic F. Bigio from B-C Graphics. **23-25:** Sketches by Greg DeSantis, inked by John Massey. **26, 27:** Sketches by Fred Holz, inked by Arezou Katoozian Hennessy. **29-33:** Sketches by George Bell, inked by Stephen A. Turner. **35-41:** Sketches by Fred Holz, inked by John Massey. **42-45:** Sketches by Jack Arthur, inked by Frederic F. Bigio from B-C Graphics. **47:** Sketches by George Bell, inked by Frederic F. Bigio from B-C Graphics. **49-51:** Sketches by William J. Hennessy Jr., inked by John Massey. **53-55:** Sketches by Fred Holz, inked by Elsie J. Hennig. **57-61:** Sketches by Fred Holz, inked by Elsie J. Hennig. **63-71:** Sketches by George Bell, inked by Elsie J. Hennig. **75-77:** Sketches by George Bell, inked by Frederic F. Bigio from B-C Graphics. **79-83:** Sketches by Fred Holz, inked by Walter Hilmers Jr. from HJ Commercial Art. **85-91:** Sketches by Greg DeSantis, inked by Walter Hilmers Jr. from HJ Commercial Art. **93-99:** Sketches by George Bell, inked by John Massey. **101-111:** Sketches by William J. Hennessy Jr., inked by John Massey. **113-117:** Sketches by Jack Arthur, inked by Elsie J. Hennig. **118-125:** Sketches by Roger Essley, inked by Frederic F. Bigio from B-C Graphics.

Index/Glossary

Time-Life Books Inc. offers a wide range of fine recordings, including a *Big Bands* series. For subscription information, call 1-800-621-7026, or write TIME-LIFE MUSIC, Time & Life Building, Chicago, Illinois 60611.